FERNS, JOHN

A. J. M. SMITH

TWAYNE'S WORLD AUTHORS SERIES

A Survey of the World's Literature

CANADA

Joseph Jones, University of Texas, Austin

EDITOR

A. J. M. Smith

TWAS 535

A.J.M. SMITH

By JOHN FERNS

McMaster University

TWAYNE PUBLISHERS
A DIVISION OF G. K. HALL & CO., BOSTON

Published in 1979 by Twayne Publishers,
A Division of G. K. Hall & Co.
All Rights Reserved

Printed on permanent/durable acid-free paper and bound
in the United States of America

First Printing

Frontispiece photograph of A. J. M. Smith

Library of Congress Cataloging in Publication Data

Ferns, John, 1940-
   A. J. M. Smith.

   (Twayne's world authors series ; TWAS 535 : Canada)
   Bibliography: p. 136-41
   Includes index.
   1. Smith, Arthur James Marshall, 1902-
2. Authors, Canadian—20th century—Biography.
PR9199.3.S55147Z65   811'.5'2 [B]   78-27486
ISBN 0-8057-6377-5

To Gill, Tom, Betsy and Carolyn

Contents

About the Author

John Ferns was born in 1941 in Ottawa, Ontario. He received an Honors B.A. from Oxford University and an M.A. and Ph.D. from the University of Western Ontario. His doctoral dissertation concerned the poetry of Gerard Manley Hopkins.

Since 1970, Professor Ferns has been a member of the Faculty of Humanities at McMaster University, Hamilton, Ontario, where he now holds the position of Associate Professor of English. During 1976-77 he held a leave fellowship from the Canada Council while on sabbatical leave at the Centre of Canadian Studies, University of Edinburgh, Scotland.

Preface

In the developing tradition of Canadian literature, A. J. M. Smith has been a poet, critic, and anthologist of importance. This study considers these three related aspects of his literary career in turn and in terms of their interrelationship. Smith's first contribution to Canadian literature was the part he played in championing international literary modernism in Canada in the 1920s and 30s. Subsequently, as a poet, critic, and anthologist he has been important in developing a view of Canadian letters that helps define the nature of the Canadian literary tradition.

The introductory chapter of the study provides an outline of A. J. M. Smith's life necessary to an understanding of his literary career. The literary situation Smith discovered on coming of age in Canada in the 1920s is described. What Smith and his contemporaries sought to do to change that situation is also discussed.

In the second chapter, A. J. M. Smith's poetry is examined in detail. The text discussed here is his *Poems: New & Collected* (1967), Smith's fullest collection of his work. Almost every one of his 122 poems is considered. *Poems: New & Collected* is divided into six sections and each of these sections is discussed in detail. The object of the examination is to determine which of Smith's 122 poems are his best. "Like An Old Proud King in a Parable," "The Two Birds," "To Hold in a Poem," "Sea-Cliff," "The Lonely Land," "I Will Remember," "The Circle," "The Fountain," "Ode: The Eumenides," and "Epitaph" are the poems that most deserve to be regarded as A. J. M. Smith's main contribution to Canadian poetry in English.

The third chapter is concerned with A. J. M. Smith's literary criticism. The key text under consideration here is his *Towards a View of Canadian Letters: Selected Critical Essays, 1928-1971* (1973). A. J. M. Smith's literary criticism, it is argued, constitutes an important contribution to the evaluation and understanding of Canadian poetry. His critical method is described as analytical, historical, and judicial.

The fourth chapter is devoted to a discussion of selected examples of Smith's extensive work as a literary anthologist. In particular his important anthologies of Canadian poetry *New Provinces* (1936), *The Book of Canadian Poetry* (1943), *The Blasted Pine* (1957), and *The Oxford Book of Canadian Verse in English and French* (1960), his anthologies of criticism of Canadian literature *Masks of Fiction* (1961) and *Masks of Poetry* (1962), and finally his anthologies of Canadian prose *The Colonial Century* (1965) and *The Canadian Century* (1973) are considered in turn. His work as an anthologist emerges as an offshoot of his work as a literary critic and poet.

The conclusion argues that A. J. M. Smith has made a distinguished and unique contribution to the development of a literary tradition in Canada. He helped to prepare the ground for the acceptance of literary modernism in Canada, but more important, he has helped to shape and define the Canadian literary tradition itself. Smith's literary career is viewed finally as a unitary enterprise, in itself an argument in favor of tradition. His activities as poet, critic, and anthologist have been related. Their central, unifying intention has been to conserve, develop, and foster the Canadian literary tradition.

I would like to thank A. J. M. Smith for inviting me to visit him in Quebec to discuss the study with him, and the Canada Council for granting me a leave fellowship to carry out and complete my work. Susan Hackett of McMaster University deserves my thanks for sending me xeroxed material and for helping with the bibliography. Most important of all I would like to thank my wife Gill for her advice and critical comments and for her kindness in typing the manuscript. Our children Tom, Betsy, and Carolyn deserve my thanks for their patience while the work was completed.

Most of the quotations of poetry and prose by A. J. M. Smith used in this study have recently been reprinted by McClelland and Stewart in two new selections, *The Classic Shade* (1978) and *On Poetry and Poets* (1977). Quotations from *The Classic Shade* and *On Poetry and Poets* by A. J. M. Smith reprinted by permission of The Canadian Publishers, McClelland and Stewart Limited of Toronto. My thanks also go to A. J. M. Smith for his generous permission to quote any material of his not reprinted there. Finally, I would like to thank McMaster University for its support in the completion of this book.

JOHN FERNS

McMaster University
Hamilton, Ontario

Chronology

1902   Arthur James Marshall Smith born in Westmount, Quebec, November 8. Attended Roslyn Avenue School, Westmount and Westmount High School.

1918-20   With parents in London, England.

1921   Graduated from Westmount High School. Began undergraduate work at McGill University.

1924-25   Founded and edited *Literary Supplement* of *McGill Daily* with A. B. Latham and Otto Klineberg. Received B. Sc. (Arts) from McGill, 1925.

1925-26   Graduate student in English at McGill, received M.A., 1926; thesis on the poetry of W. B. Yeats.

1925-27   Founded *McGill Fortnightly Review*, which he edited with F. R. Scott, A. B. Latham, and Leon Edel.

1926-27   Teaching at Montreal High School. On August 15, 1927 married Jeannie Dougall Robins.

1927-29   Fellowship in Education at Edinburgh University, Scotland. Graduate assistant and lecturer at Moray House. Working for Ph.D. under H. J. C. Grierson. Thesis: Studies in the Metaphysical Poets of the Anglican Church in the 17th Century.

1929-30   Teaching at Baron Byng High School, Montreal.

1930-31   Assistant professor Ball State Teachers College, Muncie, Indiana as one-year replacement for teacher on leave. Received Ph.D., Edinburgh, 1931.

1931-33   Temporary two-year replacement appointment at Michigan State College, East Lansing.

1933-34   Unemployed, living in East Lansing.

1934-35   Chairman of English Department, Doane College, Crete, Nebraska.

1935-36   Instructor, University of South Dakota, Vermillion.

1936-72   English Department, Michigan State University; instructor, assistant professor, associate professor, professor, Poet in Residence until retirement.

1941   January, son Peter born. Received Harriet Monroe Memorial Prize from *Poetry* (Chicago).

1941-42   Guggenheim Fellowship to prepare anthology of Canadian poetry. Spent winter in New York, travelled to Montreal and Toronto. Spent summers in Magog, Quebec. In Toronto met E. J. Pratt, Northrop Frye, Earle Birney, Claude Bissell, Pelham Edgar, and others.

1943   *The Book of Canadian Poetry* published by University of Chicago Press. *News of the Phoenix* published by Coward-McCann, New York and Ryerson, Toronto.

1944   *News of the Phoenix* wins Governor-General's Award for Poetry.

1945-47   Rockefeller Fellowship to work on Canadian prose literature.

1945-46   Spent winter in Dorval, Quebec. February, 1946 delivered Founders' Day Address at University of New Brunswick. Spring 1946 travelled in Maritimes.

1946-47   First semester at University of Toronto. Conducted graduate seminar on Canadian history and literature with Donald Creighton.

1947   Travelled across Canada to Vancouver. *Seven Centuries of Verse: English and American* published by Scribner's, New York.

1947-48   Returned to Michigan State University. *The Book of Canadian Poetry*, 2nd edition, Gage, Toronto, 1948.

1949   Visiting professor, summer school, University of Washington, Seattle; takes over Theodore Roethke's graduate seminar in poetry.

1951   *The Worldly Muse: An Anthology of Serious Light Verse* published by Abelard, New York.

1952   Taught summer school at Queen's University, Kingston, Ontario, substituting for E. J. Pratt.

1954   *A Sort of Ecstasy* published by Michigan State University Press and Ryerson, Toronto.

1955   *Exploring Poetry* (with M. L. Rosenthal) published by Macmillan, New York.

1956   Taught summer school at University of British Columbia, Vancouver.

1957   *The Blasted Pine* (with F. R. Scott), published by Macmillan, Toronto. *Seven Centuries of Verse*, 2nd edition, revised and enlarged. *The Book of Canadian Poetry*, 3rd edition.

1958-59   Sabbatical leave from Michigan State University. Spent the winter in Cannes. Travelled in France, Italy, Greece, Germany, and Austria. Litt.D. (hon.), McGill, 1958.

1960   Taught summer school at Queen's University, Kingston, Ontario. *Oxford Book of Canadian Verse in English and French* published by Oxford University Press, Toronto.

1961   *Masks of Fiction* published by McClelland and Stewart, Toronto.

1962   *Masks of Poetry* published by McClelland and Stewart, Toronto. *Collected Poems* published by Oxford University Press, Toronto.

1965   *Essays for College Writing*, published by St. Martin's Press, New York; *The Book of Canadian Prose*, volume I published by Gage, Toronto.

1966   Received Ll.D. (hon.), Queen's University; Medal of Royal Society of Canada.

1967   Received D.C. L. (hon.), Bishop's University. *Poems: New & Collected*, published by Oxford University Press, Toronto; *Modern Canadian Verse*, published by Oxford University Press, Toronto; *The Blasted Pine* (with F. R. Scott) 2nd edition, revised and enlarged. Seminar in Canadian literature at Sir George Williams's summer institute. Received Dominion of Canada Centennial Medal.

1966-67   Visiting professor at Dalhousie University, Halifax, Nova Scotia.

1968   Received Canada Council Medal.

1969   January-May visiting professor at S.U.N.Y. at Stony Brook. Seminar in Canadian literature at Sir George Williams's summer institute. Delivered Pratt Memorial lecture at Memorial University, Newfoundland. Ll.D. (hon) Dalhousie University.

1969-70   Visiting professor at McGill.

1972   Retired from Michigan State University.

1973   *Towards a View of Canadian Letters*, published by University of British Columbia Press, Vancouver; *The Canadian Experience*, published by Gage, Toronto; *The Colonial Century* (*The Book of Canadian Prose*, volume I) and

The Canadian Century (*The Book of Canadian Prose*, volume II), published by Gage, Toronto; *Exploring Poetry* (with M. L. Rosenthal), 2nd edition, revised and enlarged, published by Macmillan, New York.

1976   May 8, Symposium held at Michigan State University in honor of A. J. M. Smith.

1976-77 Claude Bissell Professor of Canadian-American literature at University of Toronto.

1977   *On Poetry and Poets*, published by McClelland and Stewart (New Canadian Library), Toronto.

1978   *The Classic Shade: Selected Poems*, published by McClelland and Stewart, Toronto.

CHAPTER 1

Introduction

I   *The Literary Situation*

THE Canadian poet, critic, and anthologist, Arthur James Marshall Smith, was born of English parents in Westmount, Quebec, Canada on November 8, 1902. He attended Roslyn Avenue School, Westmount and later Westmount High School. He tells us that:

As early as my first high school days I was everlastingly making lists—lists of favorite books, of favorite poems, which soon developed into lists of the 'best' books, the 'best' poems—or rather, what in my slowly diminishing ignorance I thought at the time were the 'best.' My parents accused me of always having my nose in a book, and it is true that I used to read one of our English texts, *Poems of the Romantic Revival*, under my desk at school during some of the duller classes such as Geography or Latin. At home I read the exciting adventure serials in *Chums* or *The Boy's Own Annual*, to be followed soon by Stevenson and even Scott. It wasn't hard to notice that the writing in *Kidnapped* or *Treasure Island* was lighter, swifter, and more vivid than in *Ivanhoe* or *The Talisman*. So was the action, and so, I think, though I could not have put a name to it then, was the quality of the imagination. Taste was developing (in poetry too), but any principles upon which it could be based were unknown, and unconsciously taken for granted. . . .

In Westmount High and at McGill in the twenties no modern poetry (except Kipling) was taught—and little Canadian poetry (except Carman). Indeed, one of my high school teachers seeing me with a copy of Masefield's *Ballads and Poems* said, "That's rather strong stuff, isn't it?" I had to discover modern poetry for myself—more or less by chance. In the Westmount Public Library I came upon *The New Poetry* edited by Harriet Monroe and Alice Corbin Henderson, published in 1917. And here I read with delight and fascination the 'new' poetry of Ezra Pound, Wallace Stevens, T. S. Eliot, Yeats in his middle period, Conrad Aiken, and H. D. This, I think is a complete list of the poets whom I deliberately began to imitate in the earliest apprentice verses I printed three or four years later

15

in the *Literary Supplement* to the *McGill Daily* and the *McGill Fortnightly Review*. These mostly appeared under various romantic pseudonyms. Vincent Starr, Simeon Lamb and Michael Gard are some I remember.[1]

Right away we can see A. J. M. Smith's love of literature, his development of a sense of critical discrimination, and his dawning enthusiasm for modern poetry. Indeed, an awareness of his related interests as anthologist, poet, and critic emerges naturally from this passage.

Together with his collaborator and friend F. R. Scott, A. J. M. Smith is rightly regarded as a central figure in the development of the modern movement in Canadian literature. Just as he was about to enter high school, and just as the First World War was about to commence, two literary events took place in Canada that indicate the crossroads in Canadian literature that would preoccupy Smith and his contemporaries at McGill a decade later. In 1913, Wilfred Campbell's *Oxford Book of Canadian Verse*, which enshrined the work of the Canadian poets of the nineteenth century, was published, and in 1914 Arthur Stringer published a volume of verse called *Open Water* which espoused, for the first time in Canada, the cause of modernist free verse.

Literary revolutions are not completed in a day. The Victorianism of Campbell's anthology persisted in Canada through the First World War and into the 1920s. After the war, which Canada had helped to win, the brash self-confidence of jingoistic literary boosterism also emerged. Victorianism and self-conscious Canadianism were the features of Canadian literary life that Smith and his McGill contemporaries sought to attack in such journals as the *Literary Supplement* of the *McGill Daily* (1924-25), the *McGill Fortnightly Review* (1925-27), the *Canadian Forum* (1920-   ), and the *Canadian Mercury* (1928-29). In the *Literary History of Canada*, Professor Monro Beattie describes the kind of Canadian literature against which Smith and his McGill friends rebelled:

Worst of all, the versifiers of this arid period, having nothing to say, kept up a constant jejune chatter about infinity, licit love, devotion to the Empire, death, Beauty, God, and Nature. Sweet singers of the Canadian out-of-doors, they peered into flowers, reported on the flittings of the birds, discerned mystic voices in the wind, descried elves among the poplars. They insisted upon being seen and overheard in poetic postures: watching for the will-o'-the-wisp, eavesdropping on "the forest streamlet's noonday song," lying like a mermaid on a bed of coral, examining a bird's nest in winter, fluting for the fairies to dance, or "wandering through some silent forest's aisles." John Garvin's anthology *Canadian Poets* (1916, revised 1926), in which appear most of these instances, abundantly demonstrates that poetry in Canada as the 1920's opened was dying of emotional and intellectual anemia.[2]

This kind of attenuated Victorianism was sustained by a prissy, coterie cosiness sharply satirized in F. R. Scott's now-famous poem "Canadian Authors Meet." Smith himself has said that this poem sums up very well the atmosphere when he began to write:[3]

> Expansive puppets percolate self-unction
> Beneath a portrait of the Prince of Wales.
> Miss Crotchet's muse has somehow failed to function,
> Yet she's a poetess. Beaming, she sails
>
> From group to chattering group, with such a dear
> Victorian saintliness, as is her fashion,
> Greeting the other unknowns with a cheer—
> Virgins of sixty who still write of passion.
>
> The air is heavy with Canadian topics,
> And Carman, Lampman, Roberts, Campbell, Scott,
> Are measured for their faith and philanthropics,
> Their zeal for God and King, their earnest thought.
>
> . . . .
>
> O Canada, O Canada, Oh can
> A day go by without new authors springing
> To paint the native maple, and to plan
> More ways to set the selfsame welkin ringing?[4]

What this parochial Victorianism had in common with the nationalistic literary boosterism of the Canadian Authors' Association, an organization which had been founded in 1921, was an absence of any real standards of literary excellence. Victorianism and Canadianism both limited the sensibility in unfortunate ways and were therefore likely to produce the second rate. This A. J. M. Smith pointed out in an essay which concluded his critical arguments in favor of literary modernism in the 1920s. Smith's article

"Wanted—Canadian Criticism" appeared in the *Canadian Forum* in 1928. In it he argued that even the good Canadian poet seemed likely, in the heady, nationalistic days of the 1920s:

. . . to succumb to the blandishments of an unfortunate popularity, the sort of popularity that appears to be at the command of any poet who hammers a vigorous rhythm out of an abundant assortment of French and Indian place-names. If you write, apparently, of the far north and the wild west and the picturesque east, seasoning well with allusions to the Canada goose, fir trees, maple leaves, snow shoes, northern lights etc., the public grasp the fact that you are a Canadian poet, whose works are to be bought from the same patriotic motive that prompts the purchaser of Eddy's matches or a Massey-Harris farm implement and read along with Ralph Connor and Eaton's catalogue (*TVCL*, 168).

A. J. M. Smith's initial purpose then as a poet and critic was to espouse and further the cause of literary modernism. This meant attacking Victorianism and jingoistic Canadianism in favor of modern diction and technique and the achievement of high standards of literary excellence.

II   *The History of a Movement*

A. J. M. Smith went with his parents to England in 1918. He was at the Cenotaph in London when the armistice was declared, just three days after his sixteenth birthday. During his visit to England he visited Harold Munro's modern poetry bookshop.[5] He returned to Canada in 1920 and graduated from Westmount High School in 1921. In the same year he entered McGill University in Montreal. His friend Leon Edel describes Arthur Smith as he knew him during his McGill days:

Smith, when I first met him, was a slim youth of medium height, with fine dark-brown hair which he combed back; usually a few strands fell over his forehead and his gold-rimmed spectacles, so that he looked like the young Yeats. He carried himself with an excess of politeness that was in his English breeding . . . but he was a tempest of poetry and revolt against established hypocrisies. . . . Arthur started to study science; after a while he moved into the English Department where we would sit at the back of a classroom and pretend to listen to Cyrus Macmillan expound Shakespeare (remembered from Kittredge) while Smith wrote poems and gave me T. S. Eliot to read. . . . Smith first taught me the meaning of literature, how words could be made expressive and shaped into a poem. He made me feel the modern idiom, the use of words as this year's language shorn of old accretions of meaning.[6]

From October 8, 1924 until March 11, 1925, Smith edited, together with his friends A. B. Latham and Otto Klineberg, a *Literary Supplement* to the university's newspaper *The McGill Daily*, which appeared on Wednesdays as an independent four-page tabloid.[7] It was followed (November 21, 1925-April 27, 1927) by the *McGill Fortnightly Review*, on which Smith was assisted as editor by F. R. Scott and Leon Edel as well as A. B. Latham. Another friend, Lew Schwartz, acted as business manager.

The *McGill Fortnightly Review* completed the establishment of a modern movement in Canadian letters that had begun a decade earlier with the publication of Arthur Stringer's *Open Water* (1914). Its early issues emphasized the importance of mythology and symbolism in modern poetry. As well as early pseudonymous poems, Smith published in the review an analysis of T. S. Eliot's *The Waste Land* in November, 1926 entitled "*Hamlet* in Modern Dress." A month later (December 15) he included an article called "Contemporary Poetry" in which he described the advent of the modern age, the arrival in less than three decades of the motor car, the steam turbine, the aeroplane, the telegraph, the wireless, and the electric light. Technology, he argued, had caused the world to contract and the pace of life to accelerate: the modern age had witnessed a movement from stability to flux. Poetry, whether accepting or rejecting its new environment, was forced into a consciousness of new conditions. Poets had to express themselves more directly than they had in the past, and to develop new techniques of expression. Yet the New Poetry, as Smith described it, was not just a consequence of changes in form and diction; it was more immediate and less abstract than the poetry of the Victorian period, seeking simplicity and sincerity. Smith saw this revolution as having taken place in two distinct phases: first, the overturning of the worn out diction and conventional rhythms of the Victorians by the imagists and the experimenters in free verse; then the rediscovery of a living tradition in the poetry of the seventeenth century that could be recovered in the twentieth century. For Smith these two phases were related. He could see links between Rupert Brooke and T. S. Eliot in, for example, their mutual admiration for the Metaphysical poets of the seventeenth century.

Modern poetry, in Smith's view, also revealed an awareness of new developments in psychology. This enabled it both to explore the working of the subconscious and to develop new forms of expression in order to present what was discovered there. Yet Smith insisted that form and subject were not two separate entities. Any division between them or suggestion of the superiority of one over the other was false. They were one, an artistic whole in which form was the body and content the soul. Smith's dislike of division in favor of unity can be seen here. In spite of this, contemporary practioners of modern poetry were poets of disillusion. Though Smith did not say so, the optimism of the new machine age was false, the First World War having wrought its havoc as we can see so clearly in works as various as D. H. Lawrence's *Lady Chatterley's Lover,* Elgar's Cello Concerto, or Carl Nielsen's Fifth Symphony.

Smith's championing of modern poetry was deliberate and intense. In the December 1926 issue of the *Canadian Forum* Douglas Bush attacked "Can. Lit. boosterism" in an article called "Making Literature Hum." Smith joined forces with him sixteen months later with his own attack on the lack of standards in Canadian letters, "Wanted—Canadian Criticism," which also appeared in the *Canadian Forum,* in April 1928. Canadian poetry, Smith argued, was too self-conscious about its position. There were too many examples in the Maple Leaf school of Canadian poetry of artificial Canadianism of the plaid-shirted, lumber-jacking variety—in short, there was too much superficial nature poetry and too little awareness of tradition. Essentially, Smith argued for better Canadian art. "Modernity and tradition alike," he wrote, "demand that the contemporary artist who survives adolescence shall be an intellectual. Sensibility is no longer enough, intelligence is also required. Even in Canada" (*TVCL*, 169).

Smith's attack was followed up by fellow poet, Leo Kennedy, who in the short–lived *Canadian Mercury* of December 1928 attacked the way in which the worst features of Victorianism still held Canadian writers in thrall. So Smith, though regularly regarded as the central figure in "the McGill Movement,"[8] as it has come to be known, was not alone in supporting literary modernism. Although he was its chief Canadian advocate, he was part of a movement that also involved his fellow poets F. R. Scott, Leo Kennedy, and A. M. Klein. The work that best represented the efforts of the 1920s at McGill and brought them to a peak was the anthology *New Provinces* which appeared in 1936. It contained poems by Scott, Kennedy, Smith, and Klein, as well as work by the Toronto–based poets Robert Finch and E. J. Pratt, the latter already an established Canadian poet.

New Provinces, edited by Scott and Smith, was the climax of the modern revolution in Canadian letters. It proved beyond doubt that modern poetry had taken root in Canada, yet its publication was not free from controversy. Smith wrote a preface to the anthology to which Pratt objected, and Scott was forced to substitute a brief preface of his own before publication could go ahead. (Smith's rejected preface finally appeared in the journal *Canadian Literature* in 1965.) Pratt probably objected to the arrogant tone of the preface and Smith's curt dismissal of so much earlier Canadian poetry. *New Provinces* proved both a peak and a turning point in Smith's literary career. Much of what he said about the shortcom ings of pre-modern Canadian poetry in the rejected preface to *New Provinces* echoed what he had argued in "Wanted—Canadian Criticism" (1928). Yet writing in the mid-30s, a year after experiencing unemployment at first hand (1933-34), Smith's rejected preface revealed a new note of social concern. "That the poet is not a dreamer," Smith wrote, "but a man of sense; that poetry is a discipline because it is an art; and that it is further a useful art; these are propositions which it is intended this volume shall suggest. We are not deceiving ourselves that it has proved them" (*TVCL*, 173).

With the publication of *New Provinces* in 1936, it is fair to say that the work of "the McGill Movement" in creating a modern Canadian poetry came to an end. Yet the movement's influence continued to be felt in the Montreal poetry magazines of the 1940s, *Preview* and *First Statement*, which finally merged in John Sutherland's *Northern Review*. Indeed, "the McGill Movement" was responsible for establishing Montreal as the liveliest center of poetry in English in Canada from 1925 to 1950.

III   *The Making of an Anthologist*

Smith received his B.Sc. (Arts) from McGill in 1925 at the age of twenty-three. A year later he received his M.A. from the same university, writing his thesis on the poetry of W. B. Yeats. A year of school teaching (1926-27) at the Montreal High School followed. On August 15, 1927 he married Jeannie Dougall Robins to whom many of his books have been lovingly dedicated. In the same year, he left Canada for the second time, to take up a Fellowship in Education at Moray House in the University of Edinburgh. Ironically, this was the university that had been the brief and unhappy residence of the Canadian poet Bliss Carman in 1882. Smith, however, gained much more from his two-year stay in Edinburgh (1927-29) than Carman had from his unhappy year. As well as being a graduate assistant and lecturer at Moray House, he had the opportunity to work for his Ph.D. under the direction of H. J. C. Grierson, editor of a famous anthology of seventeenth-century English Metaphysical poetry from Donne to Butler. Smith's thesis, for which he received his doctorate in 1931, concerned the seventeenth-century Metaphysical poets of the Anglican church. We can, perhaps, see here the influence of T. S. Eliot.

Smith returned from Scotland to North America on the eve of the Great Depression. Like most North Americans he was directly affected by it; it hindered the establishment of his academic career for seven years, during which a series of one-year positions and replacement appointments caused him to move from Canada through the northern and midwestern United States from year to year. Luckily, he did not yet have children to support.

During 1929-30 he taught at Baron Byng High School in Montreal, the high school associated with the Canadian Jewish writers A. M. Klein, Irving Layton, and Mordecai Richler. In search of a university position, he moved the next year to take up a one-year replacement appointment as an assistant professor at Ball State Teachers' College in Muncie, Indiana. A temporary, two-year replacement appointment at Michigan State College in East Lansing (1931-33) followed; then, during 1933-34, Smith found himself unemployed, though he continued to live in East Lansing, which was eventually to become his permanent home. From unemployment he leapt to a temporary chairmanship of the English department at Doane College in Crete, Nebraska during 1934-35. This was followed by a term as an instructor at the University of South Dakota in Vermillion. In January 1936 Smith was able to return to Michigan State University in East Lansing and remain there as an instructor, assistant professor, associate professor, professor, and Poet in Residence until his retirement in 1972. He still has a house in East Lansing.

In the same year as he took up permanent residence in East Lansing, the anthology *New Provinces* appeared. This was a Canadian publication, but Smith set out deliberately to have his poetry published not only in Canada but also in Britain and the United States. He advised his fellow Canadian poets to do the same. In his view, this was the only way to attain the high standards of literary excellence that were missing from such bodies as the Canadian Authors' Association. In his article "Canadian Poetry—A Minority Report" that appeared in the *University of Toronto Quarterly* in 1939 he counselled his fellow Canadian poets thus:

Set higher standards for yourself than the organized mediocrity of the authors' associations dares to impose. Be traditional, catholic, and alive. Study the great masters of clarity and intensity—Dante, Chaucer, Villon, Shakespeare, Dryden. Study the poets of today whose language is living and whose line is sure—Eliot, Pound, the later Yeats, and Auden. Read the French and German poets whose sensibility is most intensely that of the modern world—Baudelaire, Rimbaud, and Rainer Maria Rilke. Read, if you can, the Roman satirists.

Send your verse to the best English and American literary magazines. Until you are sure that your work is acceptable there, leave the Canadian magazines alone.

And remember, lastly, that poetry does not permit the rejection of every aspect of the personality except intuition and sensibility. It must be written by the whole man. It is an intelligent activity, and it ought to compel the respect of the generality of intelligent men. If it is a good, it is a good in itself (*TVCL*, 185).

Although we can hear echoes of T. S. Eliot and Ezra Pound throughout this passage, Smith himself practiced what he preached, especially in the matter of sending his verse to non-Canadian journals. He was prepared to publish in Canadian journals he respected like *Canadian Forum*, but his work also appeared in the English poetry magazine *New Verse* and in such respected American poetry magazines as *The Dial* and *Poetry* (Chicago). In fact, his efforts as a poet were recognised by *Poetry* with the award of the Harriet Monroe Memorial Prize in 1941. In January of the same year Smith's son Peter was born.

1941 was, also, the year in which Smith began his career as an anthologist of his country's poetry. His only previous experience as an anthologist was with *New Provinces*. He had always kept lists, as he told us, of the best books and poems and his work as editor of the *Literary Supplement* of the *McGill Daily* and the *McGill Fortnightly Review* together with his collaboration with F. R. Scott on *New Provinces* doubtless developed the powers of selection necessary to an anthologist. When in 1941 he was awarded a Guggenheim Fellowship to prepare an anthology of Canadian poetry he found that the Canadian poetry of the past that he had dismissed so curtly in the rejected preface to *New Provinces* and elsewhere would have to be submitted to closer scrutiny. He spent the winter of 1941-42 reading Canadian poetry in the New York Public Library. Then he travelled to Montreal and Toronto where he met and discussed his project with such Canadian poets and critics as E. J. Pratt, Northrop Frye, Earle Birney, Claude Bissell, and Pelham Edgar. *The Book of Canadian Poetry* was published by the University of Chicago Press in 1943. It received both critical acclaim and disapproval: Northrop Frye liked it, but John Sutherland didn't.

In the same year, Smith's first volume of poems, *News of the Phoenix*, appeared, published in New York by Coward-McCann and in Toronto by Ryerson Press. The following year it won the Governor-General of Canada's award for poetry. At the age of forty-two, then, A. J. M. Smith had achieved two considerable literary successes: he published an important anthology of Canadian verse and his own book of poems won his country's highest award for poetry.

IV   Later Career

One anthology led to another. In 1945 Smith received a Rockefeller Fellowship to prepare an anthology of Canadian prose. But while *The Book of Canadian Poetry* took only two years to complete, *The Book of Canadian Prose* was to take nearly thirty. A first volume appeared in 1965 and the second not until 1973. Volume I, entitled *The Colonial Century*, covered the period up to Confederation, while volume II, *The Canadian Century*, continued to the present. Smith felt in retrospect that it was fortunate that the project had taken so long because this allowed him to include in the second volume much of the new material that was to appear in Canada in the 1950s and 60s. Smith spent the two years immediately following the war working on his prose project and travelling in Canada. The winter of 1945-46 he spent in Dorval, Quebec; then in February 1946 he was invited to deliver the Founders' Day Address at the University of New Brunswick in Fredericton. His subject was appropriately "The Fredericton Poets," Bliss Carman and Sir Charles G. D. Roberts. Through cultural-historical interests which had doubtless been sparked by work on *The Book of Canadian Poetry,* Smith was able to show the influence of the Fredericton background upon the two poets. This address further revealed his concern for the creation of a Canadian tradition.

During the spring of 1946 he toured the Maritimes and in 1947 he travelled across Canada to Vancouver. His interest in Canadian prose encouraged him to travel widely through the whole of his country. During the first semester of the academic year 1946-47 he conducted a graduate seminar at the University of Toronto on Canadian history and literature with Canada's leading conservative historian Donald Creighton. During the academic year 1947-48 he returned to Michigan State University.

Smith's work as an anthologist had taken a new turn and in 1947 Scribner's of New York published his college anthology of English and American verse, *Seven Centuries of Verse.* This work shows Smith's lively sense of the English and American poetic traditions. The following year a second edition of his *Book of Canadian Poetry* appeared. This time the "Native" and "Cosmopolitan" division of Canadian poets that had appeared in the first edition was dropped. It had angered John Sutherland, who together with Irving Layton prepared in reply an anthology called *Other Canadians* (1947), and it caused Northrop Frye to suggest that Smith's "Native"/ "Cosmopolitan" division was really a division of interest within the minds of individual poets rather than a division of Canadian poets themselves into "Native" and "Cosmopolitan" schools.

In the summer of 1949, Smith travelled to Seattle to serve as visiting professor in the University of Washington's summer school, taking over Theodore Roethke's graduate seminar in poetry. Two years later his anthology of "Serious Light Verse," *The Worldly Muse,* was published in New York by Abelard. Smith himself explains the reason why this anthology is so little known: "*The Worldly Muse* had bad luck from the start, and six months or so after its publication almost the entire stock was destroyed in a warehouse fire. A couple of brief but favorable reviews in *The New Yorker* and *The New Republic* and notices in scattered newspapers in Canada and the U. S. were all I saw."[9] The following summer he taught summer school at Queen's University in Kingston, Ontario, deputizing for English-Canada's leading poet, E. J. Pratt. In 1954, Smith's second volume of poetry, *A Sort of Ecstasy,* was published by the Michigan State University Press and by Ryerson

Press in Toronto. Its title, a phrase from George Santayana, is from a quotation that Smith has made his personal poetic epigraph: "Every animal has his festive and ceremonious moments, when he poses or plumes himself or thinks; sometimes he even sings and flies aloft in a sort of ecstasy."

Another college anthology, this time edited jointly with the American poet and critic M. L. Rosenthal and entitled *Exploring Poetry*, was published by Macmillan in New York in 1955. The following summer Smith was again travelling to teach summer school, this time in Vancouver, at the University of British Columbia. A revised and enlarged second edition of *Seven Centuries of Verse* appeared in 1957 and also a third edition of *The Book of Canadian Poetry*. More importantly, a new anthology of Canadian verse appeared in the same year. As with *New Provinces*, Smith collaborated with F. R. Scott to produce *The Blasted Pine: An Anthology of Satire, Invective, and Disrespectful Verse Chiefly by Canadian Writers*. Macmillan's of Toronto were the publishers and the anthology contained such satiric gems as Scott's "Canadian Authors Meet" and "W.L.M.K." and L. A. Mackay's "And Spoil The Child." It blew a necessary and salutary breath of satire into the stuffy closet of Canadian academic and literary life.

Sabbatical leave from Michigan State University (1958-59) allowed Smith to visit Europe. He spent the winter in Cannes in the south of France and travelled in Italy, Greece, Germany, and Austria. He began to receive honorary recognition for his work as poet, critic, and anthologist at this time. In 1958 he received an honorary Litt.D. from his *alma mater* McGill. Three other Canadian universities were to honor him in this way: in 1966 he received an honorary Ll.D. from Queen's, in 1967 an honorary D.C.L. from Bishop's, and in 1969 an honorary Ll.D. from Dalhousie. Further honors included the Medal of the Royal Society of Canada in 1966, a Dominion of Canada Centennial Medal in 1967, and a Canada Council Medal in 1968. His achievement has, thus, been widely recognized and honored in Canada.

In 1960 he taught summer school once more at Queen's University. This was the year in which his *Oxford Book of Canadian Verse in English and French*, his crowning achievement as an anthologist, was published. Such an anthology was sorely needed, the most recent *Oxford Book of Canadian Verse* having been Wilfred Campbell's anthology published in 1913. Twenty years earlier Smith had felt that a revision of this volume was long overdue; Campbell's anthology was, indeed, one of the shrines of Victorianism that Smith had attacked at the beginning of his literary career. It seemed like poetic justice that he should be invited by the Oxford University Press to replace it. It was Smith's desire to include French material that gained him the task of creating this new bilingual anthology. About one-third of the poems were in French.

Nineteen sixty-one and 1962 saw the publication of further fruits of Smith's labors as an anthologist. *Masks of Fiction*, his selection of critical essays by various authors on Canadian fiction, was published by McClelland and Stewart in 1961, while *Masks of Poetry*, a similar selection of critical essays on Canadian poetry, was published by the same company a year later. Smith's third volume, and first collection of verse, also appeared in 1962: *Collected Poems*, published by Oxford University Press. Always the critic and anthologist, even of his own work, Smith's *Collected Poems* contained only 100 carefully chosen pieces. In 1965 the first volume of his *Book of Canadian Prose* appeared and in the same year St. Martin's Press in New York published yet another Smith anthology, his *Essays for College Writing.*

Although nearing the end of his academic career as Canada's Centennial year arrived, Smith, now sixty-five, brought out a second revised and enlarged edition of *The Blasted Pine*, a third revised and enlarged edition of *Seven Centuries of Verse*, a *Poems: New & Collected* that contained twenty-two new poems, and an Oxford anthology of *Modern Canadian Verse in English and French*. All four appeared in 1967. Smith was also a visiting professor at Dalhousie University during 1966-67. He taught Canadian literature at Sir George Williams's summer institute in Montreal both in 1967 and 1969. Earlier in 1969, between January and May, he was a visiting professor at the State University of New York at Stony Brook. The same year he was invited to give the E. J. Pratt Memorial lecture at Memorial University in Newfoundland. Smith's subject on this occasion was "Some Poems of E. J. Pratt: Aspects of Imagery and Theme." He paid appropriate tribute here to English Canada's major poet.

For the academic year 1969-70, Smith returned to McGill as a visiting professor. In 1972 he retired from Michigan State University as he approached the age of seventy. The next year saw, besides a second revised and enlarged edition of *Exploring Poetry*, two new publications of his work. The second volume of *The Book of Canadian Prose (The Canadian Century)* appeared, but more important, a selection of his critical essays from 1928 to 1971 called *Towards a View of Canadian Letters* was published by the University of British Columbia Press. The "Author's Note" to this volume bore the address Drummond Point, Lake Memphremagog, Québec, the summer home where Smith had spent most of his summers after his fall and winter teaching in the United States.

On May 8, 1976 a symposium was held at Michigan State University in Smith's honor. Five papers were given by colleagues and friends: Professor Sandra Djwa of Simon Fraser University spoke on "A. J. M. Smith: of Metaphysics and Dry Bones," Professor Eli Mandel of York University, Toronto on "Masks of Criticism: A. J. M. Smith, Anthologist and Critic," Professor M. L. Rosenthal of New York University offered "Laurels for A. J. M. Smith," and Professor Leon Edel of the University of Hawaii spoke on "Mr. Smith and His Worldly Muse, A Critical Homage." Finally A. J. M. Smith's lifelong collaborator and friend F. R. Scott presented "A. J. M. Smith, A Personal Memoir."

Although Smith is now in his mid-seventies, his academic career continues. During 1976-77 he was Claude Bissell Professor of Canadian-American literature at the University of Toronto, offering a graduate seminar on Canadian criticism.

It should be clear from the foregoing account that A. J. M. Smith's literary career has involved four different though related activities. As a poet he has sought by example to produce a modern Canadian poetry employing the techniques of international literary modernism such as imagism, free verse, and symbolism, though he has always shown an acute awareness of Canadian, English, and American literary tradition. To be modern in Smith's sense, as in Eliot's, does not mean rejecting tradition; rather, it means redefining tradition. Second, as a critic he has explored his country's poetry in detail and set for it high standards of international literary excellence. Third, as an anthologist he has prepared numerous anthologies, primarily of poetry but also of prose. He has emerged in doing so as, perhaps, the foremost anthologist of Canadian literature, certainly the foremost anthologist of his country's poetry. Finally, he pursued a long career as a university teacher of literature. These four dimensions of his literary career have always been closely related. It is the first three of them, Smith's work as poet, critic, and anthologist, that the present study will consider in detail. Connections between the three related enterprises, in which Smith has consistently sought wholeness, unity, and a sense of tradition, will be discussed in detail and then summarized in the conclusion.

CHAPTER 2

The Poet

A J. M. Smith first began to publish his poems in the *McGill Daily's Literary Supplement* and the *McGill Fortnightly Review* in the mid-1920s. Subsequently his poems have appeared in well known poetry magazines in Canada, the United States, England, and even Australia: *Canadian Forum, Queen's Quarterly, Dalhousie Review, Canadian Literature, Tamarack Review, University of Toronto Quarterly, Poetry* (Chicago), *The Nation, Dial, The Adelphi, New Verse, Meanjin Verse,* and *Poetry Australia* are among them. Reviewing Smith's *Collected Poems* (1962) in the journal *Canadian Literature* the English poet Roy Fuller, former Professor of Poetry at Oxford, commented, "This collection, despite its spareness, is among the most distinguished, I believe, of this century."[1] It is clear, then, that as well as being a recognized poet in Canada, where he is regarded as one of the founders of modern Canadian poetry, his work has also received recognition in the United States and England.

Besides the poetry magazines already mentioned, a selection of Smith's work appeared in the anthology *New Provinces* (1936) which finally and firmly established modern poetry in Canada. Four volumes of Smith's verse have appeared since then. Two were separate volumes: *News of the Phoenix,* in 1943, and *A Sort of Ecstasy,* in 1954. These two were followed by two collections. *Collected Poems,* which contained 100 poems, appeared in 1962; and, in 1967, came *Poems: New & Collected* which "contains all but one of the poems in *Collected Poems* (1962), now out of print, and twenty-two new pieces."[2] This is the fullest edition of Smith's poems and it is the text upon which the ensuing discussion of his poetry will be based. The discussion is neither chronological nor developmental, but rather seeks to consider the nature of Smith's achievement as a poet by examining in turn and in detail as many

as possible of his collected poems. *Collected Poems* is divided into
six parts and each of these sections will be considered in turn. The
unity of the volume will be considered after critical discussion of
the poems in the separate sections.

I   *The Two Birds*

The first section of *Poems: New & Collected* contains twenty-
seven poems. Though many of the poems are original, Yeats's
influence can be strongly felt in some of them. The opening poem,
"Like An Old Proud King In A Parable," is a four-stanza lyric of
seventeen lines. It opens with rhymed lines in the first three
stanzas, but ends with unrhymed ones in the fourth, creating an
appropriately bleak concluding effect. The poem concerns pride,
isolation, the pursuit of the natural as opposed to the courtly life,
and the singing of poetry. Although the "bitter king" of the poem
can be seen as the poet's *persona*, he is not necessarily to be seen
as the poet himself. "O who is that bitter king? It is not I" (12).
The "bitter king" rejects "fawning courtier," "doting queen," "hollow sceptre," "gilt crown," and "counties green" and makes instead
"a meadow in the northern stone." Escape from the artificial in
pursuit of the natural is strongly suggested, an expression of Smith's
love of the Canadian landscape. Yet Smith's poetry is full of
paradox; the "bitter king" breathes "a palace of *inviolable* air / To
cage a heart that carolled like a swan" (italics added). Though the
palace is airy, it is paradoxically "inviolable"; though the heart
carols "like a swan," "the bitter king" seeks "to cage" it. Although
freedom is sought, order is required. Perhaps Smith's modernist
rejection of old and search for new forms is suggested here. The
"bitter king" will sleep alone "immaculate and gay," "With only his
pride for a paramour." This language is very Yeatsian, though the
tone has an Eliot-like impersonality.

In the final two stanzas of the poem the poet who has described
the "bitter king" speaks to us directly. His desires are similar to
those of the "bitter king":

> Let me, I beseech thee, Father, die
> From this fat royal life, and lie
> As naked as a bridegroom by his bride,
> And let that girl be the cold goddess Pride:

These desires granted, the poet

> . . . will sing to the barren rock
> Your difficult, lonely music, heart,
> Like an old proud king in a parable.

The poet's situation is analagous to the king's, but not identical to
it. The poet sings "to the barren rock," the "difficult, lonely music"
of the heart. The poem shows us the isolation and difficulty, but also
the regal nature of the poet's calling. Rejecting the artificialities of a
false society, the poet seeks a new pride in isolation in "the northern
stone." To "the barren rock" he will sing the heart's music. Smith
in this signature poem seems to be defining the Canadian poet's
situation. At the same time, he seeks to thin Canadian nature poetry
down to a new purity and toughness, avoiding descriptive excess.

"Shadows There Are," the second poem in the collection, is
difficult to understand. Of course, Smith, like Archibald Macleish,
thinks that a poem "should not mean but be." The being of
"Shadows There Are" creates a sense of the ominous, a sense of
threat and fear. The poem presents two kinds of shadow. Smith is
here, as elsewhere, preoccupied with dualism. Internal or mental
shadows are not as frightening as external ones. A difference is
seen in the poem between being (mental shadows) and seeing
(external shadows). The shadows seen by the poet are "backed on
nothing in the horrid air" (13). He is evidently more frightened by
them than he was by the shadows "in the mortal mind, / Blown by
the spirit, or the spirit's wind." The poet tries to analyse the more
fearful external shadows but ". . . try as try, I cannot limn the
form/That some of them assume where I shall pass./They grow
transparent, and as sharp, as glass." The poem begins in the
present tense, reverts to the past, and then in the final stanza
moves into the future before returning to the present. It is the
movement from future to present that intensifies the sense of fear,
just as formless, transparent shadows, "backed on nothing in the
horrid air," suddenly become cruelly tangible, "as sharp, as glass."
The poem ends frighteningly with a sense of future fear become
menacingly and inescapably present. An eerie effect, like that at
the climax of Henry James' *The Turn of the Screw*, is achieved.

Smith moves in "A Hyacinth For Edith" to literary parody; in
this case, of Edith Sitwell. However, parody is not the poem's only

purpose; deeper and more significant themes lurk beneath its satiric surface. For example, such positive symbols emerge as "the bird of ecstasy," and the "bearded sun" (14). What is suggested is that through the writing of poetry—even, in this case, of poetic parody—joy and beauty can be rediscovered and reaffirmed. The poet seeks to extract an essence of beauty and joy from the dull rain of experience: "I'll seek within the wood's black plinth/A candy-sweet sleek wooden hyacinth—" or "A new ripe fruit upon the sky's high tree,/A flowery island in the sky's wide sea" (15). With the rediscovery of joy, "the gayety of bird and fruit," returns a sense of poetry seemingly lost ". . . childish cold ballades, long dead, long mute," which fall "like cool and soothing rain" upon the ardor and pain bred of the artificial "Lurking within this tinsel paradise/Of trams and cinemas and manufactured ice." Satire upon the falsity of modern society is evident here. The poet seeks the "cool and soothing rain" of the natural. Through poetry he discovers and recovers his past:

> Till I am grown again my own lost ghost
> Of joy, long lost, long given up for lost,
>
> And walk again the wild and sweet wildwood
> Of our lost innocence, our ghostly childhood.

This is a poem of "loss and symbolic repair."[3] Through the writing of a poem which begins as mere parody, the poet recovers continuity with his past: "The bird of ecstasy shall sing again,/The bearded sun shall spring again—." This is why Edith Sitwell, whose style the poet begins by parodying, is given a present, "A Hyacinth For Edith." Not "A candy-sweet sleek wooden hyacinth" either but simply a hyacinth, as the poem's title suggests.

A. J. M. Smith, as we have suggested, is a poet of duality and paradox. Having expressed a sense of recovery, he can slip back into despair. There was after all something a little uncertain about the adjective "ghostly" in the phrase "our ghostly childhood" in "A Hyacinth for Edith." "In The Wilderness" expresses unequivocally a sense of despair, reinforced by the effect of isolation achieved by the spare, rhyming two-line stanzas. There is a sense of deprivation rather than a feeling of wholeness about the poem. The poet expresses his separation from nature and language and cannot reach heaven. Smith, as we shall see, is essentially a religious poet; the truth he seeks is a religious truth. Here he expresses a sense of denial: "His gaze is stopped in the hard earth,/And cannot penetrate to heaven's mirth" (16).

As a poet, Smith always pays careful attention to form. "The Plot Against Proteus" provides ample evidence of this. The poem is a Petrarchan sonnet which rhymes *abba, cbbc, def, def*. It was a favorite form of Gerard Manley Hopkins, whose style seems to be echoed in the last line of the octave, "While rocking fathom bell rings round and rides" (17). The poem concerns an attempt to trap Proteus, the god of change. Poetic form is one means of giving shape to experience. But although Smith uses the sonnet, one of the most intricate of poetic forms, the plot against Proteus has not been completed by the end of the poem. Smith's Prince is unable to complete his task, to catch Protean chaos in his poetic net. Smith ironically invites his Prince to let him know when the plot against Proteus has proved successful. The search for stability (a still center of religious certainty) in a world of flux is as central a theme in Smith's poetry as it is in T. S. Eliot's.

"Ode: On The Death of William Butler Yeats" is not as well known as W. H. Auden's "In Memory of W. B. Yeats," but inevitably invites comparison with that more famous elegy. Smith's is less than half as long; in fact it most closely resembles the third part of Auden's poem. Auden's elegy concludes, "In the deserts of the heart/ Let the healing fountain start,/ In the prison of his days/ Teach the free man how to praise." As with Auden's "healing fountain," Smith seeks affirmative symbols in speaking of Yeats' death. Like Auden and many other elegiac poets Smith is as concerned with life in his elegy as he is with death. In stanza one he presents us with "An old thorn tree" that "Bursts into sudden flower/" (18). In stanza two "A wild swan . . . chooses to exult," while in stanza three "The white swan plummets the mountain top." Tree and swan are familiar Yeatsian symbols, deliberately selected by Smith to honor his subject. In stanza four Smith brings these two symbols of vitality together climactically:

> The twisted tree is incandescent with flowers.
> The swan leaps singing into the cold air:
> This is a glory not for an hour (19).

It becomes clear that the poem is not so much about the death of Yeats

as it is about the capacity of poetry to overcome death. In the final
stanza the swan attains eternity:

> Over the Galway shore
> The white bird is flying
> Forever, and crying
> To the tumultuous throng
> Of the sky his cold and passionate song.

Why should the eternal song of poetry be "cold and passionate"? We
are reminded of the heart's "difficult, lonely music" in Smith's
opening poem. Despite the achievement of eternity through poetry,
Smith's "Ode" is full of signs of coldness, cruelty, and deprivation.
These are the forces that poetry seeks to overcome.

It is hard to discuss Smith's next poem "Le Vierge, Le Vivace Et Le
Bel Aujourd'hui" (after Stéphane Mallarmé), since it is, presumably,
a species of poetic translation, what Robert Lowell would call an
imitation. What drew Smith to Mallarmé's frozen swan was perhaps
the theme of "useless exile" (20), of beauty and vitality destroyed by
"earth's horror." In terms of Smith's preoccupation with contrast and
dualism, juxtaposition and paradox, the poem provides a stark
counterpoint to the "Ode." In that poem the swan was successful, it
affirmed life; here it is destroyed. Probably, Smith's pervasive
preoccupation with death also attracted him to Mallarmé's poem.

Smith's interest in Yeats and Mallarmé reveals his aesthetic
sensibility, and there is often an ivory tower element in his work. It is
not one of his strengths. "To a Young Poet" offers advice in this vein:
the young poet should seek "the worth of a hard thing done/
Perfectly, as though without care" (21). We see here that Smith
values craftsmanship in the art of poetry as much as he values
inspiration.

We have already noticed that dualism and juxtaposition are
prominent features of Smith's poetry. "Bird and Flower" is no
exception. We are confronted here with opposed Christian and
classical symbols, with the poet finding it difficult to choose between
them: "Your Christian bird and Grecian flower twirled/ In gamblers'
spirals sets a trickier stake, / Grounded, o Love, in holiness and joy"
(22). In fact, he prefers the classical. "To The Christian Doctors,"
which like "Bird and Flower" is a Petrarchan sonnet, makes this
clear, although some similarity between the classical and Christian

ideals is noticed. In both, the physical or sensational must be transcended "to burn sensation's lode,/ With animal intensity, to Mind" (23). In both these poems Smith is too heavily indebted to Yeats.

The influence of Yeats is also strongly present in "With Sweetest Heresy," especially in the opening lines of the poem: "No woman, though she's made/ In the same mould as some tall Irish queen" (24). However, as the poem progresses another influence becomes evident, that of seventeenth-century English Metaphysical poetry. This can be seen particularly in the image of "love's wise parliament." At the conclusion of the poem the poet is content with the fulfillment of sensual enjoyment:". . . in an unlearnéd frenzy and contentment/ At her white side I lie/ With sweetest heresy." Like poetry, sexual love can provide escape, fulfillment, solace, or relief.

In this context it is, perhaps, possible to view the stallions in Smith's poem of that title as symbols of sexual power. Certainly the poet's "Love" is attracted by them:

> Ah, what is it they cry to you,
> O lonely pale girl, that you stand
> So straight and so still?
> That you lift up your head
> And shake out your hair, exulting—
> Turning into the wind? (25).

Certainly, too, the opening description of the stallions is attractive and vivid. It offers us an example of Smith's writing at its best and liveliest: "Slowstepping white stallions/ Coming up out of the sea—/ Their flanks flecked with foam,/ Shining white in the sun!"

If white stallions are potent symbols of attractive beauty and sexual power, the crows in Smith's next poem seem to be the stallions' symbolic opposites. They are hollow symbols of death with "brazen throat," and "bitter unspeakable tones" (26). They resemble a man who curses "the crapulous sky/and all that is beneath." We are reminded of Ted Hughes's *Crow* poems which present a similar sense of emptiness. In the first section of *Poems: New & Collected* Smith searches for a center which cannot, as yet, be found. The poems fluctuate uncertainly between affirmation and despair.

Like "The Crows," "To The Haggard Moon" presents a feeling of despair. The moon's domain is a "bleak palace" (27) and the poet asks for the "shining meadow" of the sun. Once more we are presented with symbolic opposites, an unresolved dualism. This occurs again in

"The Swan And The Dove" which suggests that we are confronted with an insistent preoccupation. Although the poem makes no direct choice between the classical and Christian annunciations, presenting each in a separate stanza, though linking the two by means of syntactical parallelism, preference for the Christian over the classical is not difficult for the sensitive reader to discern. The ordering of the two stanzas is more than merely chronological. "The Mother of Helen shrieked," "The Mother of Jesus smiled" (28): these are the opening lines of stanzas one and two respectively. The difference between the swan and the dove is the difference between a shriek and a smile. It is hard to prefer the former to the latter. Even with this amoral kind of Yeatsian presentational poetry, choice and judgement inevitably enforce themselves as far as the reader is concerned.

Classical cruelty is again evident in "Choros" which portrays in an indirect manner the sacrifice of Agamemnon's daughter Iphigenia at Aulis which allowed the Greek fleet to set sail for Troy. The poem is replete with images of death of which "Knife-thrust of silver," the opening phrase of the third and final stanza, is the most prominent. It echoes, develops, and brings into sharper focus "Sharp beak," the opening two words of the second stanza. As with the shriek of Leda in "The Swan And The Dove," there is cruelty here too, but now we have moved from rape to human sacrifice. Yeats' admiration for the classical world overlooked its cruelty. Smith's does the same, though his shift of interest from Yeats to Eliot helped him to overcome this unfortunate predilection.

"The Ship of Gold" (after Émile Nelligan) is Smith's adaptation of the French-Canadian poet Émile Nelligan's sonnet "Le Vaisseau d'or." It is a successful, though somewhat melodramatic, rendering into English. Compare, for example:

> Que reste-t-il de lui dans la tempête brève?
> Qu'est devenu mon coeur, navire déserté?
> Hélas! il a sombré dans l'abîme du Rêve![5]

with:

> What rests at last after the hasty plunge?
> What of my lost heart's fate, poor derelict
> —Foundered, alas! in the black gulf of Dream! (30).

The effect of the French is much softer than the English. Nelligan's poem concerns the sudden loss of the ship of gold, a symbol of beauty and pleasure. This striking sense of division probably drew Smith to the poem, and many of his own poems present such symbolic contrasts.

"No Knife Needed" also explores the effects of opposites. Here we encounter the different effects produced upon the heart by smiling and frowning:

> For what is frowned upon
> Turns inward on itself
> To find its best delight
> On its peculiar shelf
>
> And so avoids incisions
> That other hearts beguile
> While holding open house
> For the smiler with a smile (31).

If "No Knife Needed" contains a seed of affirmation in the heart that holds "open house / For the smiler with a smile," "The Faithful Heart" makes a more positive movement forward. In fact, the second stanza of this two-stanza poem presents the theme of renewal, resurrection, or rebirth that we find slowly replacing the theme of division in Smith's poetry. The first stanza of the poem presents a sense of loss, but in the second stanza we move from the "O Heart" of stanza one to "My true-religious heart," which upbraids the poet's want of faith. Discovering a "true-religious" sense is what leads Smith towards spiritual recovery. The "true-religious heart" creates renewal and rebirth as she overcomes loss:

> She will not feel the frost, she'll not acknowledge death.
> She says, poor fond enthusiast, the goat foot god is slain
> But like a god, whom we shall see rise from the tomb again
> She quavers we shall know him as lusty as of yore
> And bear the vine-tipped thyrsus into the woods once more (32).

However, we cannot overlook qualifying phrases such as "poor fond enthusiast" or "She quavers" attributed to the "true-religious heart." Smith may now be moving in the right direction but the process of rebirth is not yet complete. There is still an attachment to a vitalistic, pagan symbolism that will not grant the "true-religious heart" a thoroughgoing sense of faith based upon the spirit's transcendent capacity.

"Perdrix" is Smith's translation of a sonnet by another French-Canadian poet, Paul Morin. Classical-pagan symbolism seems to have been what interested Smith: a "dun Sorceress" maintains a precarious and impermanent control over her sylvan world where "once again, in thy palace of gold leaves, / The amber Dryad the cleft cedar keeps" (33). Yet another translation follows "Perdrix," "Chinoiserie" (after Théophile Gautier). Smith shares Eliot's predilection for the French. "Chinoiserie" is a love poem and celebrates the beauty of a Chinese lady who emerges as a gentler, more attractive figure than the "dun Sorceress" of "Perdrix": "From her trellis she leans out so far / That the dipping swallows are within her reach, / And like a poet, to the evening star / She sings the willow and the flowering peach" (34).

"Chinoiserie" is followed by "To Jay Macpherson On Her Book Of Poems," presumably a compliment to the Canadian poet upon the publication of her book, *The Boatman.* Jay Macpherson's powers of imagination are praised; she is presented as a Fisher Queen "Whose golden hook makes muddy waters green" (35). Smith seeks the same transforming power in his work and it is interesting that Jay Macpherson is complimented for her sacramental imagery. Such imagery would presumably lie within the domain of the "true-religious heart," "the faithful heart."

In contrast, "Hellenica" reveals Smith's continued preoccupation with classical symbolism. It is a Pound-like lament for the transience of physical beauty, sadly elegiac and fraught with despair:

> White-throated swallows
> Are swerving over the waters
> Of Mitylene,
> But we shall see no more
> The faint curve
> Of Iope's sweet mouth (36).

This is the first stanza, and the second stanza echoes it. Spring is remembered, but it has departed. In fact, the first section of the volume ends with a short series of elegies. "To Anthea" presents the death of the poet and is addressed to an unfaithful lover. Perhaps infidelity of the beloved provokes in the poet a desire for death. Everything is evened out and rendered futile by death:

> When I no more shall feel the sun,
> Nor taste the salt brine on my lips;

> When one to me are stinging whips
> And rose leaves falling one by one. (37)

Dead, the poet will forget Anthea, her "little ears," "crisp hair," and "violet eyes"; her kisses and lies will be as futile as her tears. The elegy comes close to a self-pitying appeal.

"For Healing," is, in this context, an odd but interesting poem. It indicates a desire to be cleansed of the sensual. The poet speaks here of healing as physical purification:

> Spread your long arms
> To the salt stinging wave:
> Let its breathless enveloping
> Cleanliness lave
> Arms, breast, and shoulders,
> Sinews and thighs. (38)

One physical sensation simply replaces another. The wave is "stinging," the lover's hair is described as "whips."

"No Treasure" continues the elegiac series. It is a distasteful meditation upon the physicality of death, a far cry from the mature perspective that Smith will eventually achieve.

"The Two Birds" appropriately concludes the first section. The two birds are a catbird and "that other foul bird, my black heart." The catbird's song seems raucous and unnatural amid the beauty of the natural world, but the poet realizes that it chimes with his own dissonance. He too feels out of key with the natural world. Throughout the first section of *Poems: New & Collected* we have noticed the poet's alienation, division, and isolation. In "The Two Birds," ironically, we have a similarity between the catbird and the poet's heart, but gratingly, *both* are *opposed* to nature. The poet's heart is out of harmony with nature so it seeks a *seemingly* unnatural object in the natural world, the catbird. Of course, doubly ironic, the catbird is not in itself out of key with nature; it is the poet who imagines that it is. This doubly isolates our lonely poet who has not yet found salvation.

> The wind and the water stood still,
> And stiller than these,
> As though the whole world were crystal,
> Hovered the trees.

> Only the raucous bird was something apart,
> As alien from all these
> As that other foul bird, my black heart (40).

The formal structure of the poem should also be noted. In each stanza
the word that ends the second line is repeated (not rhymed) at the
end of the penultimate line. Pattern reinforces a sense of division.

II *Canadian Nature*

The second section consists of ten poems concerned with landscape and nature. They are imagist poems insofar as they present
precisely images from the natural world. One of the ten, "The
Lonely Land," is frequently regarded as Smith's finest poem,
indeed, as one of the best Canadian lyrics ever written. Perhaps
the essential fact about these ten poems, and what makes them
distinctive, is the way in which they present Canadian nature so
compellingly and vividly.

The first of the series, "To Hold In A Poem," provides us with
an aesthetic ideal or credo:

> I would take words
> As crisp and as white
> As our snow; as our birds
> Swift and sure in their flight;
>
> As clear and as cold
> As our ice; as strong as a jack pine;
> As young as a trillium, and old
> As Laurentia's long undulant line; (42).

Smith seeks a crispness and clarity of language that will recreate
these aspects of Canadian nature. He wants to capture their
spiritual essence. The poem is also concerned with Canadian identity. Smith seeks to express a unique Canadian essence:

> To hold in a poem of words
> Like water in colourless glass
> The spirit of mountains like birds,
> Of forests as pointed as grass;
>
> To hold in a verse as austere

> As the spirit of prairie and river,
> Lonely, unbuyable, dear,
> The North, as a deed, and forever.

Interestingly, in the light of Smith's spiritual quest, the North is presented as an eternal quality. It is "lonely" like the heart's music in "Like An Old Proud King in A Parable," but it is also "unbuyable," being a spiritual rather than a material quality. Finally, it is "dear," since it is connected with love, one of the most important qualities sought by the poet.

"Sea Cliff," the second poem in the series, is much simpler than "To Hold In A Poem." It is essentially an imagistic piece of verbal representation of the movements of the sea. Alliteration, assonance, and consonance are all employed in this creation of the sight and sound of tide waves on rock:

> Wave on wave
> and green on rock
> and white between
> the splash and black
> the crash and hiss
> of the feathery fall,
> the snap and shock
> of the water wall
> and the wall of rock (43).

The echoing effect created in the last three lines of the stanza captures the sound of water on rock. This is how Smith and his fellow modernist innovators were seeking to purify the work of earlier Victorian descriptive poets. They sought to replace verbal excess, with verbal precision.

In the second stanza of the poem, time has passed and the flood tide has ebbed. This creates a new image, so that we are presented with the kind of effect that we get in haiku, which, of course, influenced imagist poetry: an effect of one image growing out of another. After the tide has ebbed we see

> wet rock,
> high—
> high over the slapping green,
> water sliding away
> and the rock abiding,

new rock riding
out of the spray (43).

"The Creek" is another delicate and subtle work of imagistic mimesis. Smith focuses upon details in the life of the creek. In the first stanza we are shown stones, roots, wisps of straw, leaves, grass, and herbs. All are carefully described so that we are given a vivid sense of what can be seen in the creek. From images we shift to the creek's movement in the second section. Alliteration, assonance, consonance, internal rhyme, and repetition help to suggest the twists and turns of the moving creek:

. . . foamfroth, waterweed,
and windblown bits of straw
that rise, subside, float wide,
come round again, subside,
a little changed
and stranger, nearer
nothing:

these (44).

The poem is the result of sensitive perception of the kind we find, for example, in Hopkins's "Inversnaid," which "The Creek" echoes in some of its verbal mannerisms and feeling for "the weeds and the wilderness."

"The Creek" is followed by "Swift Current," which presents moving water in a different way. Where "The Creek" depends upon carefully described realistic details such as "green soaked crushed leaves/ mudsoiled where hoof has touched them," "Swift Current" depends on metaphors expressing the movement of the water. It is presented first as "a visible/ and crystal wind" and finally delineated as "arrows of direction,/ spears of speed" (45). Perhaps because the metaphors are not particularly original, the poem is not as successful as the more fully realized "The Creek." It is much easier to visualize Smith's creek than his swift current.

"Walking In A Field, Looking Down And Seeing A White Violet" is once again similar in style to the poetry of Hopkins, particularly in its use of compound epithets such as "windwafted" and "mothermilky." The "looking" and "seeing" of the title introduce the poem's concentration upon the sense of sight. The poem's form reinforces this focus. Two stanzas of thirteen and twelve lines are separated by a single line of two words, "The eye" (46). In the first stanza the poet walks through the country in late winter and perceives the "torn leaves/ and straws/ of last year's grass" (46). The second stanza reveals a shift from despair to hope, from late winter to early spring. The poet's eye perceives the renewal of life in the form of a "white violet" and the eye plays "Jackstraws" (a game like "Pick Up Sticks") to discover the shy white violet:

> to disentangle
> the skywhite skyblue
> first shy white shoot
> of a white violet
> lifting a graygreen stalk
> out of the welter
> of leafgreen grassgreen
> folded over the old
> grayblack earth's
> mothermilky
> breast (46).

The springtime earth is seen, finally, as a fertile, milk-giving mother who renews life in the spring. Interestingly, the violet too is white like milk. The poem deserves comparison with Hopkins's sonnet "Hurrahing in Harvest" which may have influenced it both in style and in the reference to the violet. Differences between the two poems are that Smith's poem presents a shift of season from late winter to early spring, while Hopkins shows us the shift from late summer to early autumn. Also, where Hopkins dramatized renewal of a religious kind, Smith only presents renewal at a natural level.

In "Wild Raspberry" (for W. W. E. Ross), we find Smith dedicating a poem to his fellow Canadian imagist poet. Compliment and dedication are visible in Smith's concentration upon the simple, natural, wild raspberry. Ross is well known in Canadian poetry for simple imagist poems of this kind. "Wild Raspberry" consists of seven short two-line stanzas. As in "Sea Cliff," where we saw the seascape at high and low tide, we see the wild raspberry before and after rain. Presenting two perspectives helps in the creation of a full, three-dimensional realization. As in "Walking In A Field . . ." sight is the sense that is concentrated on. In this case the eye feasts upon the wild raspberries "and feels refreshed" (47).

Once more, as in "Walking In A Field . . . ," nature provides renewal or refreshment. In the opening two stanzas we see the "Wild Raspberry" before the rain:

> Your ragged leaves
> are speckled with dust
>
> They are frayed at the edges
> and sticky with sunshine (47).

After rain a new view is gained which provides the refreshment revealed at the end of the poem:

> but after the rain
> gashes of red
>
> glisten
> among slipp'ry green leaves
>
> Yellow whips
> and prickly little branches
>
> are pulled into curves
> by the big berries.

The rain brings color and relief, like the rainbow, and we see the freshened reds and greens.

Seventh among Smith's Canadian nature poems is "Birches At Drummond Point" (Lake Memphremagog). This is the lakeside place in Québec's eastern townships where Smith, for years, has made his summer home. The poem is a delicate and simple realization of the poet's thought that the "slim white birches" seem to "offer a silent rebuke" or "message." When the leaves of the birches rustle, the poet listens. "What do they say?/ or seem to?" are the final questions that Smith asks himself. The poem is a simple speculative lyric in which the poet asks himself what it is that nature has to tell us.

"Tree" continues this speculative strain. Here Smith wonders about the nature of the relationship between language and nature:

> Words are ciphers
> denoting speeds and directions

> not of thought only
> but of things.
>
> I say tree
> and the rain falls
> and the sun gets to work
> and the seed breaks
> and the sprout appears
>
> and the years pass
> and here it is spring again (49).

The poem ends with an image of a boy carving a heart and a name in a tree. The return of spring is the poem's central event and ties its three interests together: language (and poetic inspiration), nature, and love are all quickened by the spring.

"The Lonely Land" is, perhaps, Smith's best and certainly his best known poem. It has the same kind of place in Canadian poetry that Tom Thomson's "Jack Pine" has in Canadian painting. In fact, "The Lonely Land" was subtitled "Group of Seven" (after that group of Canadian landscape painters) when it first appeared in the *McGill Fortnightly Review* on January 9, 1926. Smith was not satisfied with the first version of the poem and a heavily revised and much improved second version appeared eighteen months later in the *Canadian Forum* of July 1927. Still the poet was not content, and two years later the final, further improved version appeared in the American poetry magazine *The Dial* of June 1929.[6] It is the final version that will concern us here. The poem is in four stanzas of eleven, eleven, twelve, and four lines. In the first stanza we are presented with a harsh, northern Canadian lake-scape of the kind encountered in a Group of Seven canvas. Both "Cedar and jagged fir" are described as uplifting "sharp barbs," "against the gray/ and cloud-piled sky." Adjective and verb present the evergreens as harsh and menacing. The sky too is bleak in color and possibly threatens rain. From tree and sky we move to the bay of a lake which answers the sky's menace with a windswept menace of its own. Pine trees too are blowing:

> and in the bay
> blown spume and windrift
> and thin, bitter spray

> snap
> at the whirling sky;
> and the pine trees
> lean one way (50).

Explosive "b" and sibilant "s" sounds create the feeling of wind-tossed lake, sky, and trees.

In the second stanza a lonely bird sound intensifies the already bleak picture. "A wild duck calls/to her mate" and the poet goes on to describe the echo and reverberation of the duck's call on the stones at the water's edge:

> and the ragged
> and passionate tones
> stagger and fall,
> and recover,
> and stagger and fall,
> on these stones—
> are lost
> in the lapping of water
> on smooth, flat stones.

Having created his bleak picture and filled it with laconic sound, Smith tries to tell us in stanza three what kind of "beauty" this landscape possesses. He calls it "a beauty/of dissonance." The "stony strand" of the lakeshore has "resonance" and the wild duck's call is then further described as "this smoky cry." It curls "over a black pine":

> like a broken
> and wind-battered branch
> when the wind
> bends the tops of the pines
> and curdles the sky
> from the north (51).

The "smoky cry" is then likened to a branch snapped from a pine bent by the wind. Though we see in "The Lonely Land" a "beauty of dissonance" (the evergreens are sharp, the sky is gray; sky, trees, and lake are swept by wind, the duck is wild, and its unanswered call, "ragged/and passionate," is likened to a broken branch), nevertheless this beauty also has resonance and strength, a "beauty/of strength/broken by strength/and still strong." Division but persisting strength is the subject of this moving and impressive evocation. Like Archibald Lampman's "Heat," "The Lonely Land" is one of the best known and best Canadian lyric poems.

Smith's sequence of Canadian nature poems, which probably provides the collection with its strongest single section, ends with "The Convolvulus." There is word play here on "morning glory," which is a kind of convolvulus. Smith addresses the flower and asks it to express the joy of its natural being. The summertime in which the convolvulus will fully realize itself is presented as a "communion." Smith here praises the glory of nature. To the simple, narrow-throated convolvulus he says:

> Let your paean of being
> ring like a great shout
>
> distinguished
> in the diapason
>
> of the yellow sun
> and a million green shoots
>
> —in the communion of summer
> and the morning's glory.

Here the musical imagery is appropriate to the bell-shaped flower of the convolvulus. In his Canadian nature poems Smith demonstrates his ability as a poet at its best. His lyric response to the natural world is both elegant and full-blooded.

Of course, the question arises how different from or better than the Maple Leaf nature poetry that he attacked is the nature poetry of A. J. M. Smith? To compare Smith's poetry to Maple Leaf verse of the early years of the century would be futile. The real answer should involve close comparison with the nature poetry of Archibald Lampman. What will such an analysis reveal? Perhaps the difference between nineteenth-century Romantic-Victorian nature poetry and modern nature poetry is imagism. Smith's nature imagery is more precise, sharper, and harder-edged than Lampman's. From the sensuousness and suggestion of Keats and Arnold, we move to the imagistic precision of Eliot and Pound. Comparison of two passages, one from Lampman and one from Smith, reveals this

difference. Let us consider the openings of their two most famous
poems:

> From plains that reel to southward, dim,
>   The road runs by me white and bare;
> Up the steep hill it seems to swim
>   Beyond, and melt into the glare.
> Upward half-way, or it may be
>   Nearer the summit, slowly steals
> A hay-cart, moving dustily
>   With idly clacking wheels.
>
> (Lampman, "Heat")

> Cedar and jagged fir
> uplift sharp barbs
> against the gray
> and cloud-piled sky;
> and in the bay
> blown spume and windrift
> and thin, bitter spray
> snap
> at the whirling sky;
> and the pine trees
> lean one way.
>
> (Smith, "The Lonely Land")

Although Lampman's "Heat" moves deliberately from vague to
precise images, it is safe to say that Smith would be unlikely to use
a work like "dim" in any context. In line two Lampman presents
himself, while in "The Lonely Land" the self is deliberately
excluded in a characteristic imagist way. We should notice too that
Lampman's lines are longer than Smith's free verse lines and that
Lampman uses a rhyming eight-line stanza form whereas Smith's
use of rhyme is incidental in stanzas of varying length. Lampman's
picture of nature is sensuous and expansive, Smith's is hard and
precise. In part this is because they are depicting very different
scenes, yet there is a difference between Romantic-Victorian harmony with nature and modern detachment. Smith's approach to
and depiction of nature is essentially different from Lampman's,
whose "The City of the End of Things" may nevertheless have
influenced Smith's anti-materialism. For the Romantic-Victorian
poet nature could be entered into, whereas for the modern poet of
alienation or isolation nature and man stand apart from each other.

III   *The Circle and The Fountain*

The third section of the collection contains thirty-one short poems of five different kinds. First we have three poems of a satirical cast about the role of the poet, "One Sort of Poet," "Pagan," and "Three Phases of Punch." "Pagan" might more properly be called a poem of lyric celebration, but the other two pieces are certainly satirical. Indeed, "One Sort Of Poet" presents the kind of poet that Smith himself is not. Canadian poetry has seen too many poets of this kind:

> Though he lift his voice in a great O
> And his arms in a great Y
> He shall not know
> What his heart will cry
> Till the fountain rise
> In his columned throat
> And lunge at the skies
> Like a butting goat (54).

"One Sort Of Poet" is the subjective poet who depends entirely upon "inspiration" for his work. What this leads to is described elsewhere in section three in "A Dream Of Narcissus" as the "mad, inevitable goal/Of proud Romanticism!" (75).

The second kind of poem in section three is the love lyric, poems like "What Strange Enchantment," "I Shall Remember," "Field of Long Grass," and "Song (Made in lieu of many ornaments)." The first three of these are successful because of their gentleness and lyric simplicity; the fourth is less successful because of its coldness and hardness. Though it is difficult to say which of the first three is the best, "I Shall Remember" is, perhaps, the most moving in its combination of nostalgic memory and love. The bird is frequently an image of poetic inspiration in Smith's poetry. Here the curving movements of "A lonely swallow" are connected in the poem with the curves of a lover's smile. The result is a sympathetic love poem that shows us Smith's poetry at its simplest and best:

> I shall remember forever
> A lonely swallow swerving
> Over a dusky river,

> Sweeping and solemnly curving
> In long arcs that never
> Stirred the still stream,
> For so your smile
> Curves in quiet dream (61).

Long vowels and the "s" alliteration create a feeling of peace and gentle love.

The third group is the most difficult to categorize, consisting of ten poems, some of which are symbolic in technique and some exploratory or speculative in theme. In this loose grouping we could number poems like "The Circle," "The Fountain," "A Little Night Piece," "Nightfall" (Fin de siècle), "The Trance," "A Narrow Squeak" (Variations on a theme of Anne Wilkinson), "The Mermaid," "Poor Innocent," "A Dream of Narcissus" and "Universe into Stone."

The first two, "The Circle" and "The Fountain," are the best poems in the third section. They are worth considering in some detail because they reveal Smith's work as a poet at its best. Both show his preoccupation with elegance of expression and perfection of form, and produce chiselled, eighteenth-century clarity. "The Circle" is written in six four-line, *abab*, ballad stanzas. The circle presented in the poem is the circle of the seasons: in stanza one we have summer, in stanza two fall, in stanzas three and four it is winter, in stanza five spring has returned, and stanza six returns us just prior in time to the moment described at the end of stanza one. The poem can thus be seen to be moving forward or backward in time, and this ambiguity helps to create the circle image. Compare the opening and the closing stanzas:

> Over me the summer drips,
> And over me the wind cries;
> The tree above me sways and dips,
> The bird above me sings, and flies.
>
> . . . .
>
> And now the oozing summer drips
> Through heavy days of slow delight:
> The tree above me sways and dips,
> The bird above is poised for flight (62).

Balancing stanzas describe summer at either end, stanzas two and five symmetrically depict autumn and spring, while stanzas three and four present winter. Balanced architecture of form helps to reinforce our sense of the image of the circle. Throughout the poem Smith's language is sensuous and simple, but it contains a good deal of repetition that again enforces an impression of circularity as, for example, in the lines "Of amethyst and drifting snow/ Of drifting snow and amethyst."

"The Fountain" is an equally interesting example of Smith's poetic art. While "The Circle" concerns the cycle of the seasons, "The Fountain" presents an image that transcends seasonal circularity, developing a symbol of transcendence over time. "Enchanted," "immortalized," "metamorphosis," "form," and "transfigured" are words used in connection with the fountain which, like one of Shakespeare's sonnets, is presented as having the power to overcome time: "And Time is fooled, although he storm" (63). Though there is no direct or even indirect hint of this in the poem, the fountain seems to represent the art of poetry itself.

The fountain's water is first presented as "flowery spray" and the fountain is then likened to "some enchanted tree of May." Fountain water is like a tree in bloom. But more than this, the tree when compared to the fountain is "Immortalized in feathery frost/ With nothing but its fragrance lost." A "white metamorphosis" has taken place. All that the tree has lost is its fragrance. "White metamorphosis" reminds us of Smith's love of the English Metaphysical poets of the seventeenth century, as Marvell's "green thought in a green shade" comes to mind.

Transcendence, which is one of Smith's central preoccupations as a poet, is developed more fully in the poem's second stanza: "Through Autumn's sodden disarray/ These blossoms fall, but not away." The water blossoms of the fountain continue to fall even in autumn, but, unlike leaves, they do not disappear. Instead, "They build a tower of silver light/ Where Spring holds court in Winter's night." The fountain is offered as a symbol of endurance in the face of seasonal transience. Finally, the fountain becomes an image of light in darkness: "And while chaotic darkness broods/ The golden groves to solitudes,/ Here shines, in this transfigured spray,/ The cold, immortal ghost of day." We are left with a final, haunting image of the nighttime fountain that reminds us in darkness of the day. In the phrase "golden groves" there is a direct echo of Hopkins's "golden-grove unleaving" in his poem "Spring and Fall." Though it is tempting to see the fountain as a symbol of poetic art itself with its ability to give permanence to the transient, it is best, finally, to leave the poem on the natural level that the actual words of the poem present. We can see how Smith's Canadian nature poems have here blossomed into an ability to reveal a beautiful, artificial object as natural.

The fourth group consists of Smith's translations from French-Canadian and French poets. There is also an adaptation from Cavalcanti's *Ballata IX* called "A Pastoral." There are six pieces altogether; besides "A Pastoral" we have "May Song" (after Jacques Prévert), "Brigadier" (A song of French Canada), which is very well done, "The Hippopotamus" (after Théophile Gautier), "The Hunter" (after Eloi de Grandmont), which is amusing but not as good as "Brigadier," and finally "Pastel" (after Théophile Gautier). It is difficult to discuss Smith's adaptations and translations without entering into detailed comparisons between Smith's English versions and the French originals. Smith's translations are done with the aid of a dictionary and the help of other translations which he can often convert into English poems. John Glassco, D. G. Jones and F. R. Scott are other English-Canadian translators of French-Canadian verse.

We now come to the fifth and final grouping, which contains eight poems that could be called "love parodies." They concern erotic love but could hardly be said to be serious in the way that the earlier poems are. They include "The Sorcerer," which is surely the best of them, "Ballade Un Peu Banale," with its reference to Eliot's (Gautier's) hippo, "The Adolescence of Leda," which is not really a "love parody" at all, "They Say," "Souvenirs Du Temps Bien Perdu," a piece of Betjemanesque eroticism, "An Iliad For His Summer Sweetheart," "Thomas Moore and Sweet Annie," and "The Country Lovers." As indicated, "The Sorcerer" is the best of these poems, the lightest and wittiest. The qualities of form and language evident in "The Circle" and "The Fountain" and that characterize Smith's work at its best are present in "The Sorcerer."

Smith likes the four-line ballad stanza and "The Sorcerer" is one of many of his poems that employ this form. Like "The Fountain," it concerns transformation, but here the subject is treated wittily and ironically. Interestingly, the poem also concerns renewal or regeneration, but this theme too is lightly treated. The opening of the poem reveals that "There is a sorcerer in Lachine" who has the power "for a small fee" to put a spell upon the poet and his beloved. It is amusing that the sorcerer should live in Lachine, Québec, since that name means "China," where the original explorers thought they had arrived. It is certainly an appropriate place for a sorcerer to come from. This sorcerer has special powers: "He will transform us, if we like, to goldfish:/ We shall swim in a crystal bowl,/ And the bright water will go swish/ Over our naked bodies; we shall have no soul" (69). The point of the soullessness mentioned at the end of the stanza becomes clear at the end of the next stanza. The sorcerer is a priest of love who usurps the functions of a Christian priest. As a goldfish, the poet's beloved will no longer have to attend confession: "In the morning the syrupy sunshine/ Will dance on our tails and fins./ I shall have her then all for mine,/ And Father Lebeau will hear no more of her sins."

The sorcerer, it is now clear, has been engaged comically to create a world entirely devoted to love for the poet and his beloved. Ironically, this is love *in* a goldfish bowl. If the sorcerer will grant the poet and his lover this contained sphere of love, the poet plans to forget both "intellect and lust." "Come along, good sir, change us into goldfish./ I would put away intellect and lust." In the last two lines of the poem Smith shows us that light verse can be serious as well as comic. In fact, as noted, Smith has edited an anthology of "Serious Light Verse" as if to prove this point.[7] The poet would "Be but a red gleam in a crystal dish,/ But kin of the trembling ocean, not of the dust." Clearly the poet's wish that he and his love become goldfish is absurd and silly and the poet too sees that it is. Nevertheless, even within this comic wish the poet seeks to become "kin of the trembling ocean, not of the dust." How is this possible? Surely a poem concerned with regeneration should be serious and not take this absurd and comic form. How can lovers transformed to goldfish by a sorcerer in Lachine become "kin of the trembling ocean" and avoid death, "the dust"? They gain vitality through the light, comic idea itself. It is precisely the idea that renewal and the reacquisition of vitality must be deadly serious that the poem is out to defeat. "The Sorcerer" may not, finally, be as profound and satisfying as "The Circle" or "The Fountain," or as moving in a simple way as "I Shall Remember," yet it is without doubt the most successful of Smith's "love parodies." The reason for this is that it avoids crassness. The light manner expresses a serious concern which the poem delightfully reveals should not always be treated solemnly, since its attainment requires a comic sense.

In the third section we find the heart of Smith's achievement as a poet. Poems like "The Circle" and "The Fountain," clearly demonstrate Smith's formal control. Beyond this they display his ability to use language with a direct and simple elegance. Although in some of his more contorted and elusive efforts Smith courts obscurity and sometimes fails to avoid it, at his best, in poems like "I Shall Remember," "The Circle," "The Fountain," and "The Sorcerer," he achieves resonance and clarity. Like Hopkins, whose poetry has also been charged with obscurity, Smith is at heart a simple poet. With this simplicity comes a delicate sensuousness that expresses feelings of gentleness and love. Though his work sometimes seems hard, cold, and stony, Smith is able to express tenderness, as in his love poem "Field Of Long Grass." Indeed, love seems to be the central concern of the poems of the entire third section:

> Light is like the waving of the long grass.
> Light is the faint to and fro of her dress.
> Light rests for a while in her bosom.
>
> . . . .
>
> Then she begins to walk in my heart.
> Then she walks in me, swaying in my veins.
>
> My wrists are a field of long grass
> A little wind is kissing (66).

IV   *The Claims of Reality*

The fourth section of *Poems: New & Collected* contains seventeen poems, most of which are satirical. The bureaucracy, materialism, and technology of the twentieth century make it inevitable that the poet will be a satirist, supporting older communal and individual values. Poetry depends upon the real communication of feelings and ideas that mass society by its nature denies.

The opening poem is ironically titled "Noctambule." At its center is a satiric attack upon the mass-produced illusions of the twentieth century: "Perhaps to utilize substitutes is what / The age has to teach us" (92). In this little night walk we first encounter a "pneumatic moon," "—Blown up to bursting, whitewashed white, / And painted like the moon —." This false moon "is only an old /

Wetwash snotrag—horse-meat for good rosbif —." Perhaps, the
poet's nausea comes through a little too distastefully and grimly
here. In this modern world of the artificial substitute we encounter
further "the loud / Unmeaning warcry of treacherous daytime"
which issues "like whispers of love in the moonlight." We become
confused in the modern world to such an extent that daytime
blaring is accepted as nighttime love whispers. In this world a lion
mews and a mouse roars. But the mouse suffers shellshock and
twitches his skin in "rancid margarine." There is once more a sense
of physical nausea provoked by social and spiritual disorder. Ironically remembering the circumstances that inspired Yeats's famous
poem "The Lake Isle of Innisfree," Smith likens the mouse's eye to
a lake isle in a florist's window. Now we have "Reality at two
removes, the mouse and moon / Successful" (92). Thus, in modern
technological society we have the triumph of the false and the
cowardly. It is a nasty picture. Smith's poem presents modern
society as a Dali-like surrealist painting. Though the satiric intention is clear, the poem nevertheless leaves the reader with an
extremely unpleasant feeling.

"Far West," the second poem in the section, once again features
"Reality at two removes." We are shown a cowboy film, perhaps
taking place in a London cinema, and an adolescent girl's confused
response to it. A "boy friend" seems to be "at her" as well:

> Among the cigarettes and the peppermint creams
> Came the flowers of fingers, luxurious and bland,
> Incredibly blossoming in the little breast.
> And in the Far West
> The tremendous cowboys in goatskin pants
> Shot up the town of her ignorant wish (93).

In the second stanza of the poem we see how the young girl's
perception of reality is confused by cinematic romance: "In the gun
flash she saw the long light shake / Across the lake, repeating that
poem / At Finsbury Park." The poem the girl read in school was
Tennyson's Song from *The Princess,* she remembers "The long
light shakes" and "Our echoes roll from soul to soul."

An echo of gun and poem is "drowned in the roll of the trams—."
The girl is alone. Who would have heard her thoughts anyway?
"Not a soul. / Not one noble and toxic like Buffalo Bill." There is
no one to equal Buffalo Bill, the subject of her sexual fantasy. We

see that what Smith is satirizing here is mass media's pop star cults that confuse the young and fill their minds with specious images. The last stanza of the poem suggests in its sensual imagery that the Western film has filled the girl's mind with the confused images of sexual fantasy.

One of the central concerns of Smith's poetry is the theme of regeneration and renewal. In "Resurrection of Arp" this theme is treated ironically. Arp is reborn, but the experience has no meaning for him; he treats it as a mere technological triumph. The experience leaves him unchanged, and he is not reborn in any significant emotional or spiritual sense. Unlike the resurrection of Christ, Arp's merely material resurrection is, in fact, diabolical: "On the third day rose Arp / out of the black sleeve of the tomb; / he could see like a cat in the dark, / but the light left him dumb" (94). Arp is like one of T. S. Eliot's "hollow men," a kind of Mr. Eumenides. This modern resurrection is a cruel parody of the Christian original, through which Smith expresses his hatred of the modern world of meaninglessness. When Arp comes to testify his tongue will not work. His voice rattles and rolls, heresies scattering "like ninepins," and his resurrection is a "sell-out." In fact, it is a hellish event. The resurrection of Arp is the coming of a modern anti-Christ like Yeats's "rough beast": "When they turned down the gas / everybody could see there was / a halo of tongues of pale fire / licking the grease off his hair." Christian images are confused and distorted in this poem: instead of the descent of a Holy Dove, "a white bird / fluttered away in the rafters," and instead of the Biblical rushing of mighty wind, "people heard / the breaking of a mysterious wind (laughter)."

Arp then speaks a language initially described as "majestic beautiful wild / holy superlative believable" (95). We are attracted but instantly there is satiric deflation. This language is "undefiled": "by any comprehensible / syllable / to provoke dissent / or found a schism. . . ." Arp is now presented as a modern day "holy-roller" preacher, a diabolical Billy Graham. The poem concludes:

> After the gratifyingly large
> number of converts had been given receipts
> the meeting adjourned to the social hall
> for sexual intercourse (dancing) and eats.
>
> Arp talked to the reporters:
> on the whole, was glad to have cheated the tomb,

> though the angels had been 'extremely courteous',
> and death, after all, was only 'another room'.

What finally is the point of this odd satire? Presumably it is another attack on modern illusions, in this case scientific technology's desire to defeat death. Arp's resurrection is unreal, a stage managed illusion with tickets and reporters, indeed all the trappings of a modern sporting event, with as little real meaning or significance.

"A Portrait, And A Prophecy" is linked in theme to "Resurrection of Arp," since it too is concerned with religion. Once again Smith's concern is with hypocrisy or illusion, with the mask. The character satirized in "A Portrait, And A Prophecy" undergoes a false conversion: he pretends "Penitence" and "Innocence" but, in fact, remains egocentric. As the poem announces, this character's chief preoccupation is "Himself." "Indeed, he has sinned! and of his many sins the chief / That mortal sin, Himself" (96). The religious hypocrite is portrayed in the first four stanzas of the poem, while the fifth stanza contains the poem's prophecy. The character satirized is seen variously in the portrait as "a smiling falsifier" and as "a young Victoria of wax and wood." In the prophecy it is suggested that the religious hypocrite will degenerate morally, "grow from not-so-good to bad." He will become "Untruthful, nasty, secretive, and sad." He will drive his mother to madness and "end by growing up just like his dad." The portrait becomes a prophecy of the power of environmental determinism, a bleak prophetic picture, indeed.

Smith continues his satires on modern culture by turning from religion to literature. In his next short sequence of four poems his subject is poetry, either the abuse of poetry or false attitudes towards it. The first of these poems is called "On Reading An Anthology Of Popular Poetry." Smith is upset at the way in which poetry is used simply as a vehicle for the expression of personal pain. There is no concealment, no distance, no impersonality—in short, no art—in the anthology of popular poetry that Smith describes:

> Cries from the stitched heart
> In soft melodious screams
> The sweet sweet songs that start
> Out of alluvial dreams?
> The old eternal frog

In the throat that comes
With the words *mother, sweetheart, dog*
Excites, and then numbs (97).

In conclusion, Smith wonders whether there isn't another catharsis than poetry for personal pain. Why must every "Saul of Tarsus" seek to "pant himself into a Paul"? Presumably because every poet seeks to transform or come to terms with himself through poetic expression. Of course, as Smith suggests, this personal preoccupation does not always make for good poetry.

"Stanzas Written On First Looking Into Johnston's *Auk*" is also concerned with poetry, inspired by the Canadian poet George Johnston's book *The Cruising Auk* (1959). It is perhaps a parody of Johnston's comic style. When Smith writes in the final stanza, "And I myself am a whimsical chap, / A Betjeman manqué, if not a Donne," (98) it is hard to know what his satiric object is. Is he mocking George Johnston or presenting an ironic view of himself? One of the problems with Smith's satires is the occasional uncertainty they create about their objects. The title, of course, suggests an amused glance at Keats' famous sonnet "On First Looking Into Chapman's Homer." In this case, however, we seem to be travelling in realms of madness rather than in "realms of gold."

The third piece in this short sequence deals with another book of Canadian poetry, Irving Layton's anthology of Canadian love poems, *Love Where the Nights are Long* (1962). Layton's gross style is Smith's satiric object in the opening lines of the poem. The poet in "The Devil Take Her—And Them" claims ironically that he would rather play golf or read *Playboy* than make love to his mistress because her attention has been deflected from him by Layton's anthology. For weeks the poet's lover has been "sighing for all the lyrical feats / Of poets from Montreal between the sheets" (99). This should not be taken seriously or as in any way true or real. Its object is simply to make fun of the erotic atmosphere in which Layton moves and breathes.

As we noted earlier, Smith spent many years as Poet in Residence at Michigan State University. In his poem "On The Appointment of Ralph Gustafson, Esq., As Poet In Residence At Bishop's University" he creates a satire of academe to celebrate his fellow Canadian poet's appointment to a similar position. The "Groves of Academe" have generally, Smith observes, been ruled over by "The leaden Owl" of solid scholarship. But the appointment of a Poet in Residence brings renewal. "But now, a marvel! a green laurel springs/And from its topmost bough a linnet sings" (100). Though presented in a comic-satiric manner, Smith's concern with regeneration appears once again. The creation of a Poet In Residence is ironically seen to cause the convocation of professors to dance: "Lo! as the black Professorate advance/In solemn Convocation, see, they dance!" (100). Would that this were the usual result of the creation of such positions.

Section four concludes with eight further poems on various subjects, most of which are treated satirically. Satire, indeed, is the fourth section's driving force. First, in a two-line piece called "The Taste Of Space," Smith presents the kind of sensuous distortions suggested by Marshall McLuhan, who is described as putting "his telescope to his ear" to detect "a lovely smell" (100). Even lightly treated, Smith's subject remains the distortions and illusions created by modern society.

In the next poem, "Souvenirs Du Temps Perdu," dedicated to his McGill contemporary, the Henry James scholar, Leon Edel, Smith recalls a Paris New Year's Eve. Repetition helps to create the lurching, drunken effect of the poem. There is also parody of the way that literary allusions crop up in drunken, student conversation. We bump into references to Brooke's "Grantchester," Yeats's "Lake Isle of Innisfree," and Eliot's *The Waste Land,* all mixed together with popular song. The poem finally and simply is an ironic memory of college days.

"My Lost Youth" also glances backward. There is self-satire involved here as Smith looks back at his past and a remembered love relationship. It is an April evening with the fragrance of hyacinths in a drawing room as the diffident poet converses with his young lady, who smokes and speaks of poetry and love. Smith creates the atmosphere well. The diffident poet finds it hard to look directly at the young lady and thinks of his birthplace and his past. This is the most directly autobiographical of Smith's poems:

> I thought of my birthplace in Westmount and what *that* involved
> —An ear quick to recoil from the faintest 'false note.'
> I spoke hurriedly of the distressing commonness of American letters,
> Not daring to look at your living and beautiful throat (102).

The young poet's uneasy combination of intellectual pretentiousness and shyness is well captured. He models himself upon literary images:

'She seems to be one who enthuses,' I noted, excusing myself
Who strove that year to be only a minor personage out of James
Or a sensitive indecisive guy from Eliot's elegant shelf.
'What happens,' I pondered fleeing, 'to one whom Reality claims. . . ?'

The poet seeks to be a Jamesian or Eliotic anti-hero, someone like
Prufrock perhaps, for it is Eliot's "The Love Song of J. Alfred
Prufrock" that this poem recalls. Like Prufrock, the poet here is
"indecisive" and ponders "fleeing" from a potential love encounter.
Yet he is claimed by the reality of time and age. It is a middle-aged
self, thirty years on, that the final stanza of the poem presents: "I
teach English in the Middle West; my voice is quite good;/My
manners are charming; and the mothers of some of my female
students/Are never tired of praising my two slim volumes of verse"
(103). The satirist, Smith feels, must not spare himself.

"Quietly To Be Quickly *Or* Other Or Ether" (A Song or a Dance) is
simply a piece of ironic word play, perhaps a satiric treatment of the
theme of distortion itself. To further the range of Smith's satiric
subjects we have "Political Intelligence," which submits politics to a
deserved satiric scrutiny.

The following poem, "What The Emanation Of Casey Jones Said
To The Medium," sounds satiric, but is, in fact, a fairly serious
meditation on time and death. Finally, we have "Astraea Redux
Keewaydin Poetry Conference" (For Kim and Doug). It lacks the
perspective of "My Lost Youth" and is too personal, too sentimental,
and finally too embarrassing and maudlin. The chief success, then, of
this fourth section of satiric poems is probably "My Lost Youth."
Smith's sense of self-irony is exact and incisive there. It should be
remarked in conclusion, though, that Smith is a much better lyric
poet than he is a satirist. Satire is not his forte; his friend F. R. Scott is
much better at it.

V   *News Of The Phoenix*

The eleven poems in the fifth section are again mainly satirical.
Political and social satire is Smith's main emphasis here, rather than
the poetry and religion of section four.

"Son-And-Heir 1930" shows us what bourgeois parents of this
period hoped for from their male offspring. They cast their son in the
role of a Hollywood capitalist, who will give "his old dad/Market tips,
and cigars on Father's Day," (114-115) and send "his Mother

telegrams and roses" (115). The poem is shot through with cinema terms to reflect the parents' mental creation of a Hollywood success story life for their son. In stanza one we have "Instinct censors any real, as too forlorn, / Preview of coming attractions"; "Angels sing / like press agents the praises of their lamb" (114). The poor child is featured as "the smirking star." In the parents' "scenario" the son is seen "Striding over the very veldtlike veldt / In a bandolier full of Kodak films." Seen as a star by his parents, the son is actually carrying films in his parents' image of him. He seems to be literally becoming a film. "They make him up in the attractive role / Of a he-god in the next episode."

After five stanzas describing these parental expectations, Smith asks, "Who will turn the lights up on this show?" The parents are in the dark, unable to accept the claims of reality. What Smith is satirizing in the poem is the infamous "American dream" which, as his date "1930" suggests, must have been especially bankrupt at that time. The parents' eyes are accustomed to cinematic illusions about their son; they cannot face reality:

> . . . their eyes, used to horse opera, cannot grow
> Used to an ordinary sonofabitch
>
> Like you or me for a son, or the doom
> We discern—the empty years, the hand to mouth,
> The moving cog, the unattended loom,
> The breastless street, and lolling summer's drouth,
>
> Or zero's shears at paper window pane. . . .
> And so forth and so forth and so forth.
> Let us keep melodrama out of this scene,
> Eye open to daylight, foot on the firm earth (115).

Smith asks us finally to accept the claims of reality and not fill our minds with romantic illusions.

"News Of The Phoenix" is the poem that gave its name to the title of Smith's first volume of poems. In it he again satirizes the modern state. It is rumored that the phoenix, the mythical figure of regeneration and renewal that so preoccupies Smith, is dying; some say that the phoenix is actually dead. Of course, the mythical phoenix does not die but renews itself every thousand years. The death of Smith's phoenix is reported in the language of the modern totalitarian state:

Dead without issue is what one message said,
But that has been suppressed, officially denied.

I think myself the man who sent it lied.
In any case, I'm told, he has been shot,
As a precautionary measure, whether he did nor not (116).

The message that the phoenix is dying or dead, and even worse,
dead without issue, is suppressed and officially denied. Even the
modern police state it seems does not want to leave man without hope
and so attempts to deny the death of the phoenix which symbolizes
hope and renewal. Yet in stanza two the poet says that he thinks that
the officially denied message was probably a lie. Does this mean that
the phoenix lives? Then we learn that the man who delivered the
message has been shot whether he lied or not. Perhaps it is that the
modern state wants no news of the phoenix at all, even if the news is
bad. The modern state seeks to suppress hope, imagination, regeneration, the qualities that the phoenix represents. Modern society lacks
any coherent mythology or sense of hope; that we no longer hear even
"news of the phoenix" is perhaps the bleak meaning of Smith's poem.
Possibly too the phoenix symbolizes art. Smith thinks that it lives but
the modern state kills those who make bleak pronouncements about
the death of art; it wants the mass of people to believe that life is rosy.
It is difficult to interpret the poem's meaning exactly because we
cannot be sure what Smith wants the phoenix to represent.

"Eden's Isle," which is dated November-December 1956, is about
the Suez Crisis in which the British Prime Minister Anthony Eden
attempted an abortive military action to prevent Egypt's nationaliza-
tion of the Suez canal. The poem opens with a quotation mark which
is never closed. (Presumably this is a typographical error; the
quotation marks ought logically to close at the end of the first line of
the poem, which is a quotation from Shakespeare's *The Tempest*,
"The Isle is full of noises.") In the poem, Eden's Isle is Great Britain,
the Eagle the United States of America, and the Sphinx, Egypt.

Britain is an isle "full of noises" of political conflict. Images in
stanzas two and three suggest the death of empire. The Suez action
was Britain's last attempt to assert her imperial authority:

The sea wind in the oak trees
Shrieks like a prophet of death
Or whines as a man will wheeze
Who fights for his last breath.

> The cliffs crumble to chalk
> Where the breakers thunder and thud
> The vessels moored at the dock
> Are drained of their life blood (117).

In the final stanza we see that the power of the U.S.A. symbolised as the Eagle overshadows Eden's Isle. As a result of this the Egyptian Sphinx "smiles a stone smile." Britain would have required the support of the U.S.A. to be successful in her Suez action and such support was not given: "The Eagle rides on the storm;/ His shadow blots out the Isle:/ And in the East, the immovable form/ Of the Sphinx smiles a stone smile." Smith's style and use of allegorical symbolism is reminiscent of a poem like Yeats's "The Second Coming."

"Ode: The Eumenides," also has a modern political and social pertinence. The Eumenides are the vindictive figures of fate in Aeschylus's *Oresteia*. In his ode, Smith implies that we have only just begun to reap the whirlwind of our collective crimes in the twentieth century. The Ode is presented in three sections. In the first, Smith wonders if we could escape the revenge of those so casually killed if we could return to innocence. Then follows the refrain, *"These times indeed/ Breed anguish."* In the twentieth century we have lost both religion and honor. How can we return to these life sustaining realities?

> Betrayed by the cold front
> And the bright line
> How shall we return
> To the significant dark
> Of piety and fear
> Where holiness smoothed our hair
> And honour kissed us goodbye? (118).

"The significant dark" is a beautiful way to express the nourishing sense of religious awe, but the succeeding images of holiness and honor are too tritely maternal.

The opening and closing refrain of the poem's second section strikes at the heart of our modern, gluttonous materialism in three of the best lines in Smith's poetry:

> *How shall we ask for*

> *What we need whose need*
> *Is less, not more?* (119).

The benign and creative influence of T. S. Eliot on Smith's poetry is beautifully and strikingly evident here. Beyond any anxiety about influence, it is the kind of creative influence that leads to fresh originality and continuity of feeling and thought. The two stanzas of section two suggest the punitive threat of Russia and China. Our secular society has created its proper punishment in the form of Marxist atheism. In "Ode: The Eumenides" we have a fine combination of feeling and thought. Smith's moral meaning and his emotional response to our society's emptiness unfold simultaneously. The two stanzas of section two of the Ode are two of the finest in his poetry:

> Now that the dragon seed
> Grows tall and red, we
> Harvest in the field
> Sharp sheaves, and see
> The reaper felled
> By what we took such care
> To sow so straight.

His language here is direct and simple and has the kind of eighteenth-century clarity that his best work possesses:

> Our secular prayer,
> Sincere and passionate,
> Created its own
> Power and instrument
> And will. There is none
> However innocent
> In heart or head,
> That shall escape
> The stench of the dead
> Emptied and butchered hope
> In lives and deaths made
> Meaningless froth.

The final section of the poem is grim in the extreme. It suggests that we will reap what we sow. We will be unable to return to the wood of innocence but "have a date in another wood, / In the

stifling dark, / Where the Furies are" (120). We will, in fact, be
killed by ourselves; our death will be a kind of suicide because we
have forsaken "piety and fear." Smith expresses the horror of
self-confrontation in the poem's last lines:

> The unravelled implacable host
> With accurate eyes levelled
> Wait in the enchanted shade.
>
> Where we spilled our bloodshot seed
> They wait, each patient ghost
> My ruined son.
>
> *The furies lift the veil—*
> *I know that face!*

The form and language of "Ode: The Eumenides" have a force that
make the poem easily Smith's most successful poem in section five,
and one of the most successful works in his poetic canon. It speaks
with a race's soul's recognition of having sowed the seeds of its own
destruction. "Ode: The Eumenides" is clear, direct, and tragically
telling in its account of how Western man has ruined himself. As
Thomas Hardy is so often quoted as saying, "If a way to the better
there be, it demands a full look at the worst."

"A Soldier's Ghost" tells movingly how a soldier's sacrifice is
frequently an act of love. It is an elegiac rather than a satiric poem:

> Can a memberless ghost
> Tell?
> These lost
> Are so many brother bones.
>
> *The hieroglyph*
> *Of ash*
> *Concedes an anagram*
> *Of love.* (121)

Similarly, "The Dead" concerns our modern burden of consciousness. The dead in this century we still have with us. As with
Wilfred Owen's war poems, the poetry here is in the pity. The
father depicted in the poem:

> . . . lives,
> Indeed, but might as well be dead
> As these anonymous statistics,
>   Whose loves
> Were just as kind as his, whose lives
> Were precious, being irreplaceable (123).

Smith's recognition of the uniqueness of each individual human being is moving and provides his poem with a fitting conclusion. It reminds us of the Scottish poet William Soutar's moving poem, "The Permanence of the Young Men."

Smith's concern in section five with political and social satire continues in a pair of poems "Business As Usual 1946" and "Fear As Normal 1954." The first poem concerns the "orderly de-control" that followed the end of the Second World War in Canada, but by the second poem we are in the depths of "Cold War brinkmanship." The first poem expresses the smug sense of Canadian remoteness from the actual European arena of the Second World War. "Here we are safe, we say, and slyly smile" (124). In the distance are "the spears/ That clank—but gently clank—but clank again!"

The second poem of the pair opens with words that closed the first. By 1954 we ask, "But gently clank? The clank has grown/ A flashing crack—the crack of doom" (125). The fear of nuclear holocaust and radiation poisoning leads to a hideous parody of Hopkins's presentation of the Holy Ghost (in "God's Grandeur") in the shape of an H-Bomb's mushroom cloud which "Over the bent world broods with ah! bright wings." The poem ends in further literary parody, this time of Yeats's "Leda and The Swan": "We guess it [the H-Bomb] dazzles our black foe;/ But that it penetrates and chars/ Our own Christ-laden lead-encaséd hearts/ Our terrified fierce dreamings know."

"The Common Man" is a social satire in five parts. Here Smith shows how in modern society the common man, like Dr. Johnson's common reader, has disappeared. As a result of the lack of community of mass society, he has become an abstraction, the politician's object:

> He was the public good, the target one
> At whom each sugar-coated poison-spraying gun
> Was levelled. Whatever was done was done

To him. He was the ear communiqués
Addressed, the simple mind for which the maze
Of policy was clarified. His praise

Was what the leaders said was their reward.
To pierce his heart the patriotic sword
Was dipped in ink and gall and flourished hard (128).

The loss of a proper regard for the common man cuts the heart out of society.

"The Bridegroom," another poem in five parts, also attempts to grapple with the claims of modern reality. The bridegroom, like the common man, is an everyman who sets forth to experience modern life. The poem resembles Archibald Lampman's "The City of the End of Things" in its presentation of hideous mechanization. From sensuous contact with his bride, "significant dark", the bridegroom descends a long hillside to experience the hell of the mechanical world. Will he ever be able to return properly to her after the horror of this experience? A similar experience is dramatized in the character of Ewan in Lewis Grassic Gibbon's novel *Sunset Song*. We feel that Smith's bridegroom will be brutalized in the same way that Ewan was by his military experience. Modern man, in D. H. Lawrence's phrase, has become a monkey minding a machine. "The Bridegroom" is Smith's most Lawrentian poem:

> How shall he ever return now
> Up the steep hillside
> To his innocent bride?
> He shall take on his creased brow
> The sweat of these.
> The only peace
> That he shall know
> Is love of these: but it will stop
> Far short of hope (131).

The "these" referred to are the victims of mechanization whom the bridegroom will love out of charity, though his hope for the world is lost. We end up wishing that he had never left his bride and sought the modern, scientific world; ". . . the significant dark / Of piety and fear" would have been better.

Section five ends with an adaptation from the Hungarian of

Ferenc Juhász entitled "At Twenty-Six." The poem affirms "the ineffable / Quality of man" (133) in the face of the many degradations he suffers in the twentieth century. Smith clearly shares the humanism of Juhász.

To summarize, section five consists mainly of social satires. The best of them is indisputably "Ode: The Eumenides" because of its power and force.

VI *Epitaph*

Most of the twenty-four poems in the sixth and final section are concerned with the related subjects of death and religion. The section begins with "Prothalamium" and ends with "Epitaph."

"Prothalamium" is about the transience of human life; it solemnly announces the section's central concern with death. The poem contains allusions to John Webster's play *The Duchess of Malfi* ("Malfy"), Shakespeare's *Hamlet* ("the Danish battlements") and the sermons of John Donne, "that preacher from a cloud in Paul's" (136). The two plays and Donne's sermons all concern death. The poem shows how we receive the summons of death. In the opening stanza we are presented with an image of the slow erosion of a wall, an image subtly realized in four of Smith's finest lines:

> Here in this narrow room there is no light;
> The dead tree sings against the window pane;
> Sand shifts a little, easily; the wall
> Responds a little, inchmeal, slowly, down (136).

In the second line there is a muted reminder of Tennyson's "Mariana" ("the blue fly sung in the pane") and the word "inchmeal" is brilliantly suggestive in its evocation of the erosion of the wall of Hopkins' "leafmeal" in his poem "Spring and Fall."

At the end of the poem the summons of death has increased its insistence. The dead tree now fumbles at the pane, trying to get in like the hand in Emily Brontë's *Wuthering Heights*. Now a bell tolls, a sound unheard in stanza one, and we have, "Ceiling dripping and the plaster falling, / And Death, the voluptuous, calling."

In the section's second poem, "The Two Sides Of A Drum," we discover that "eternity and time / Are the two sides of a drum" (137). There is a delicate reminder of the seventeenth-century poet

Henry King's famous poem *The Exequy:* "my pulse, like a soft
drum, / Beats my approach / Tells thee I come." This poem is
followed by an adaptation or translation "*From the Hungarian of
Zoltán Zelk*" called "When I Was A Thrush." Again the subject is
time and death. The thrush has avoided the sparrow-hawk all
summer, but now sits in a wintry tree: "I'm waiting to awaken. I /
Am waiting to die!" (137). The idea of death as a form of renewed
life will be developed further in the section, especially in the
profound and moving "Epitaph" which concludes the volume.

The death theme recurs in "Journey," where the poet

> . . . asks of heart
> To bear a braver part
> When death draws nigh.
>
> And for reply,
> Heart moveth not. And all is said (138).

There is no sense of awakening or renewal here. Death is bleakly
viewed as the end of life.

"The Bird" calls to mind poems like Saint-Denys-Garneau's
"Bird Cage" and Hopkins's "The Caged Skylark." It is much more
optimistic than "Journey" was, since it sees the possibility of
spiritual liberation in death. The body is the bird's cage and when
"One" (God presumably) opens the door of the cage the spirit will
fly free. Just as Wordsworth's children come "trailing clouds of
glory," so the spirit flies back to an original place of freedom once
the door of the body's bird cage is opened:

> Free then of the flesh hood
> And the cage of bone,
> Singing at last a good
> Song, I shall be gone
>
> Into that far and wild
> Where once I sang
> Before the flesh beguiled,
> And the trap was sprung (139).

It seems clear from "Journey" and "The Bird" that Smith ap-
proaches death from various points of view. These two poems
portray first a pessimistic and then an optimistic response to death.

"To Henry Vaughan" expresses Smith's sense of Vaughan's love of life, yet glad acceptance of death:

> Yet art thou Homesick! to be gone
> From all this brave Distraction
> Wouldst seal thine ear, nail down thine eye;
> To be one perfect Member, die;
> And anxious to exchange in death
> Thy foul, for thy Lord's precious, breath,
> Thou art content to beg a pall,
> Glad to be Nothing, to be All (141).

We have here Smith's sense of the Christian paradox, the idea of dying into life, of leaving this earth to attain a heavenly life, what Smith in the chapter of his Ph.D thesis on Vaughan calls "the final dying into an ecstasy of God-filled life. . . ."[8]

We have noted already that many of Smith's poems are elegiac. "In Memoriam: E.J.P." (26 April 1964) is his elegy for English Canada's most famous poet, E. J. Pratt. Pratt's death occurred in the spring and Smith is once again faced with a paradox: "How shall we speak of the death of an old poet in April?" April is, or should be, the time of renewal. As Smith reveals in his most successful poems, "only the simplest words have meaning" (142). Then follows a statement of poetics:

> Poems, which are the spiritual blood of a poet,
> Renew themselves in an eternal April,
> And renew us also who take them into ourselves.
> Thus the poet becomes as one of the gods
> And in the church of the poem we communicate.
> We receive a benison—
>   Not necessarily holiness,
>   Not necessarily wisdom—
>   Rather a flood of ferocious joy
> That springs like a fountain in the heart
> And cannot be dammed or diverted or turned off (142).

These are not particularly *poetic* lines. In fact, they are rather flat in rhythm and read like a prose statement. Yet we do not doubt that Smith means what he says. We have first the idea of poetry as the poet's "spiritual blood," the finest and highest expression of himself. Poems are deathless; phoenix-like, they eternally renew themselves. They are what live of the mortal poet, words by which he will be remembered and which allow him to communicate with a wider audience than his family or immediate group of friends and colleagues. Poetry is like communion in Smith's view, since poems also renew those "who take them into ourselves." The poet becomes *like* a god whose poems are his eternal body or "spiritual blood," "And in the church of the poem we communicate." Here the reader meets the poet and receives a gift, neither necessarily holiness nor wisdom but the "flood of ferocious joy" of the poet's "spiritual blood" that wells unceasingly from the heart. This is one of the fullest descriptions of poetry that Smith provides us with and it is clear that he sees poetry as similar to Holy Communion. In the second part of the poem Smith indicates that Pratt has given of himself, died, and therefore reached beyond need. Dead, he cannot know that we, the living who still have needs, praise him. The poem concludes:

> Giving him nothing,
> We take all:
> *Praise to the Giver of All!*
> *Praise to the End!* (143).

Dead, Pratt does not need our praise, but it does not follow that the gift of an elegiac poem is nothing. Fair enough we take from him but Smith's poem is also a gift. *"Praise to the Giver of All! / Praise to the End!"* are moving words, as Smith reveals his sense of God and the importance of praise.

"The Offices Of The First And The Second Hour" is a religious meditation, somewhat reminiscent, in style and technique, of T. S. Eliot's "Ash Wednesday" or *Four Quartets*. The office of the first hour is "TO ABJURE;" the office of the second hour is "QUIETLY TO ATTEND" (144). The religious poet here first seeks to reach the light of God beyond darkness and then realises that he must wait for God's light which is, indeed, beyond "darkness and light" as we, in a worldly way, understand them. Smith sees that he must, "Quietly . . . attend the unfolding light's stark / Patience, inhuman and faithful like a weed or a flower, / Empty of darkness and light." In this poem Smith seeks unity with God.

"The Cry" is a little like one of Hopkins's sonnets of desolation though it is not as personal. In the octave Smith uses a first person plural. Here the style and contorted syntax are quite like Hopkins: ". . . Is it this / Granite overgrown or no sweetsmelling vale / Only to gain? No more?" (145). But in the sestet, Smith (unfortunately) detaches himself from the experience of religious anguish and shows us instead of his own suffering:

> A tired boy, at midnight probing a sore,
> Sobs, lifting the word from a touched lung.
> Where are the flashing limbs? They bloom no more.
> Only the thin dust stiffens the pricking tongue.
> He cries out *Jesus shew me thy grass thy green*
> *Else how shall I keep this thing I have not seen!* (145).

The religious anguish is genuine and is doubtless Smith's own (how else could he dramatize it), but it might have been more fully confronted, indeed, even overcome if it had been faced directly and squarely as Hopkins faces his religious anguish in his sonnets of desolation. By trying to detach himself from his own experience Smith leaves himself in a limbo similar to that of T. S. Eliot's hollow men.

"Canticle of St. John" (after Stéphane Mallarmé) seeks religious nourishment and honors God: "Watering my root / Dip in salute" (147). "Calvary," the next poem, shows us the power of the crucified Christ who even on the cross has "flung the moving lance / Of a world-destroying gale" (147). "Calvary" is appropriately followed by another religious poem called "Good Friday." Again Christ's power is acknowledged:

> This day upon the bitter tree
> Died one who had he willed
> Could have dried up the wide sea
> And the wind stilled (148).

The poem ends in prayer and we feel the full force of Smith's Christian belief here where in other places it seems uncertain:

> What answering meed of love
> Can this frail flesh return
> That is not all unworthy of
> The god I mourn? (148).

Smith's poems show us the flood and ebb tides of his religious life. In some places he seems agnostic, even atheistic; here we have one of his fullest expressions of love of Christ.

It is right that "Good Friday" should be followed by "Beside

One Dead." Here the phoenix myth used elsewhere is given a Christian transformation, in which Smith's preoccupation with regeneration, renewal, and resurrection finds its fullest and most resonant articulation. Like Mary Magdalen and the disciples on the first Easter Sunday we encounter:

> The opened tomb
> and the Lord gone:
> Something whole
> that was broken (149).

Smith seeks wholeness throughout his work; here he finds it in the form of the risen Christ. This poem expresses the completion of Smith's Christian pilgrimage.

   Poems: New & Collected could have ended here, but, in fact, there are eleven further poems that continue Smith's meditations upon death and religion. "The Shrouding" is filled with recognition of what has been perceived in "Beside One Dead." If Christ's breaking was restored to wholeness, so can ours be: "But stand up in your shroud / Above the crumbling bone, / Drawn up like one more cloud / Into the radiant sun" (150).

   There is reverence for the dead in the next poem, "In the Churchyard At South Durham, Quebec" (Circa 1840). The poet celebrates a woman who once walked beside us but now lies beneath the ground. She was a particularly holy person who "seemed to breathe the purer air / Of paradise" (151) even while she lived. Therefore, the poet asks us, since he reveres her life, to

> Tread softly: tenderness and grace,
> High promise and sweet trust
> Perfume this quiet place
> And sacred dust (151).

   In stanzas like this and in poems like "The Shrouding," "Beside One Dead," and "Good Friday," Smith's poetic language is direct, simple, and sincere, demonstrating how much he learned from his study at Edinburgh of poets like Donne, Herbert, and Vaughan. Indeed, he manages to continue in his own way their seventeenth-century tradition of religious awe and reverence.

   Of less importance is "What Is That Music In The Air?" It concerns an elusive voice heard by the poet, "A voice from the heroic dead" (152). But the poem itself is elusive in meaning and consequently of less importance than the moving sequence of religious lyrics which immediately precede it. Nor is "Metamorphosis" as good as the religious lyrics previously discussed. It concerns transience, the exchange of life for death and death for life, but does little more than play with this theme. Also, "My Death" seems solipsistic after poems like "Beside One Dead" or "The Shrouding." Of death Smith writes:

> I am the food of its hunger.
> It enlivens my darkness,
> Progressively illuminating
> What I know for the first time, yes,
> Is what I've been always wanting (154).

Rather livelier, "The Wisdom Of Old Jelly Roll" concludes:

>   . . . 'Cry at the birth,
> Rejoice at the death,' old Jelly Roll said,
> Being on whisky, ragtime, chicken, and the scriptures fed (155).

Old Jelly Roll is presumably the jazz pianist Jelly Roll Morton, who expresses the folk attitude to death of the New Orleans "Oh Didn't He Ramble" or the Irish wake. The Christian paradox is forcibly brought home here.

"On Knowing *Nothing*" is morbidly preoccupied with death. One wishes that Smith had fully accepted the Christian view and stuck to that, but instead he seems intent to show us all possible attitudes to death. Modern fear and vicarious fascination are two of the least useful attitudes to death. Thus we have the not very good poetry of:

> The surgeon's jab, a woman's thigh
> Give blank surcease
> For short or long.
> I cannot let the hollow
> Interval alone,
> But pick it like a scab
> To probe the wound within—
> As deep, as nothing, as the grave (156).

"Watching The Old Man Die" is, we must suppose, honest, but

it is also almost as morbid as "On Knowing *Nothing.*" Presumably, the poet is contemplating the death of his father, though it might be any old man. It doesn't much matter, which tells badly against the poem. Poetry, as Smith has indicated earlier, should reach beyond the merely confessional. It is not without purpose that we speak of the impersonality of great art. Smith's Christian poems about death have this impersonality. Beside them, "Watching The Old Man Die" is a disappointment:

> The body cannot lie.
> I savored my own death
> And wept for myself not him.
> I was forced to admit the truth
> It was not his death I found grim
> But knowing that I must die (157).

"The Archer" more successfully expresses the poet's fear of death. The archer is, perhaps, a figure for the poet himself; his arrow "a burning thought," a poem which seeks to allay or destroy his fear of death:

> So for a moment, motionless, serene,
> Fixed between time and time, I aim and wait;
> Nothing remains for breath now but to waive
> His prior claim and let the barb fly clean
> Into the heart of what I know and hate—
> That central black, the ringed and targeted grave (158).

"Speaking About Death" (Blues for Mentor Williams) then under-cuts this whole subjective preoccupation with such terse lines as: "Speaking about death. / What a waste of breath they said / What a waste of breath / *There is nothing to say*" (159).

It is with a real sense of elevation that we arrive at "Epitaph," the final poem in the volume. "Epitaph" is a mature, wholly serious work of art and it reveals the fruitful result of Smith's careful study of the English Metaphysical poets. It is also the culmination of Smith's work as an elegist. An elegiac strain runs through his collected poems, but "Epitaph" is the best of them. It has the kind of maturity that we find, for example, in Ben Jonson's famous elegy "On His First Son" or Andrew Marvell's "Horatian Ode upon Cromwel's Return from Ireland." While Smith scorns and satirizes the limitations of modern society in other poems, in "Epitaph" he reveals his acceptance of the terms of human life. He asks his reader not to weep on "this quiet stone," his gravestone, since,

> I, embedded here
> Where sturdy roots divide the bone
> And tendrils split a hair,
> Bespeak you comfort of the grass
> That is embodied me,
> Which as I am, not as I was,
> Would choose to be (160).

"Epitaph" reveals a complete and mature response to life and death. The gravestone is described as "quiet," since death involves the attainment of peace by the poet. He is appropriately "embedded" in the earth, and does not reject this condition. His bones are divided by "sturdy roots," the adjective "sturdy" suggesting the poet's awareness, indeed celebration, of the strength of continuing life. Smith's Metaphysical wit is subtly evident in line four that recalls Donne's "bracelet of bright hair about the bone." Here we have pedantic tendrils splitting a hair. Smith's love of language is at its finest here as he restores vitality to cliché. Tendrils split a hair on the poet's corpse as, like the "sturdy roots," they thrust forward in assertion of life. We are forced to consider "minute particulars" here, the detail of the action of death that is confronted and accepted rather than turned away from and rejected. "Bespeak" is an archaism appropriate in this poem, since it reinforces our sense of the time-laden nature of the subject. The grass can provide comfort, since it is the poet's body in another form. "Embodied" also echoes "embedded" in line two and subtly suggests the birth out of death theme so frequent in Smith's poems. The poet accepts his new condition; in fact, he would choose it. The poem is cumulatively dramatic, leaving the final union of thought and feeling, the achievement of fresh perception, to the last two lines. Archibald Lampman's famous lyric "Heat" does the same. It is this kind of influence (of Lampman on Smith) that creates the continuity of a vital poetic tradition in Canada. But we must go back beyond Lampman's "Heat" to George Herbert's "The Collar," a poem whose climax Smith discussed in his Ph.D.

thesis, to find the roots of a Canadian tradition in English. The creation of a real Canadian tradition does not involve the rejection of English or French traditions. *Poems: New & Collected* ends strongly with "Epitaph."

CHAPTER 3

The Critic

I Synoptic

ALTHOUGH not all of A. J. M. Smith's literary criticism concerns Canadian literature, the bulk of his best critical writing has concerned the literature of his country. This may, at first, seem surprising in one who is an avowed internationalist, received his doctorate from a British university, and spent most of his academic life teaching at a university in the United States. But as a Canadian poet Smith has been deeply and intensely interested in the literary tradition of Canada. In fact, his literary criticism has helped to reveal the shape and provide a definition of Canadian literary tradition.

Smith's best critical writing is gathered in a recent volume entitled *Towards a View of Canadian Letters: Selected Critical Essays, 1928-1971* (1973). This book of essays, like *Poems: New & Collected*, is divided into six sections. The structure of the book is itself interesting: the first four sections provide a history of Canadian poetry, the fifth Smith's critical principles, and the sixth a "Self-Review" of his own poetry and some personal reflections "On the Making of Poems."

The first section of the book, "Synoptic," contains two essays. The first essay, "A Brief History of Canadian Poetry," is Smith's introduction to *The Oxford Book of Canadian Verse in English and French* (1960) and is a distillation of his thinking about Canadian poetry over the twenty-year period since he had begun work in 1941 on the first *Book of Canadian Poetry* (1943). The second essay grows out of the first. It is called "Eclectic Detachment: Aspects of Identity in Canadian Poetry" and it first appeared in the journal *Canadian Literature* in 1961. It attempts to describe the special situation of the Canadian poet.

"A Brief History of Canadian Poetry" begins by presenting
Canadian poetry as "a branch of English or French poetry and to
some extent also, particularly in the work of contemporary writers,
of American poetry."[1] Poetry is described as "the art that most
directly and intimately expresses and evaluates the compulsions of
life and its environment" (3). Smith sees Canadian poetry as evolv-
ing through three phases: colonial, national, and finally into a
cosmopolitan stage of development. Canadian poets, in Smith's
view, are divisible into two schools: native poets and cosmopolitan
poets, those who have sought to express the uniqueness of the
Canadian environment and those who have sought to write about
universal themes:

> . . . Canadian poetry is and always has been a record of life in the new
> circumstances of a northern transplantation. And the record takes on
> significance and attains a more than local relevance as technical proficiency
> makes possible a more intense and accurate expression of sensibility.
>   From earliest times Canadian poets, both French and English, have
> held, consciously or unconsciously, to one of two distinct and sometimes
> divergent aims. One group has made an effort to express whatever is
> unique and local in Canadian life, while the other has concentrated on
> what it has in common with life everywhere (4).

The earliest backwoods poets were of the first group and their
inspiration was Robert Burns. They were direct and realistic versifiers like Standish O'Grady and Alexander McLachlan. But there
were also more "literary" imitators of Lord Byron and Tom Moore.
The first English-Canadian poets of any importance, in Smith's
view, were Charles Sangster and Charles Heavysege, and the first
to describe Canadian nature in any real detail was Charles Mair. In
1864, in his preface to one of the first anthologies of Canadian
poetry in English, the Reverend Edward Hartley Dewart argued
that "A national literature is an essential element in the formation
of national character" (5). The three Charleses, Smith argues, were
the first to provide this. Yet the first truly *Canadian* poetry in
Smith's view, was the work of Isabella Valancy Crawford. He
describes her poem "Malcolm's Katie" (1884) as:

> the first, and not one of the least, of the few poems that can be really
> called Canadian, because its language and its imagery, the sensibility it
> reveals, and the vision it embodies are indigenously northern and west-
> ern, a product not of England or the States but of Canada (8).

Smith sees the development of French-Canadian poetry as (to a considerable extent) parallel to that of English-Canadian poetry. He interweaves discussion of poetry in each language through the course of the essay. Octave Crémazie was the father of French-Canadian poetry though he later turned against his own nationalistic and patriotic work. He was followed by Louis Fréchette, one of the first Canadian poets to achieve recognition outside Canada. Poets such as Pamphile Le May, William Chapman, and Nérée Beauchemin developed the *terroir* school of landscape poetry at the same time that Charles G. D. Roberts, Bliss Carman, Archibald Lampman, and Duncan Campbell Scott "established a national school of reflective nature poetry and achieved a standard of technical excellence unattained in Canada before and only rarely equalled since" (10). The goal of these poets, both English and French, was "to interpret nature and the impingement of nature upon the sensitive mind in ways that were peculiar to their northern locale" (12). The influence of these poets, especially in English Canada, had in Smith's view, a "dazzling" and "stupefying" effect. For two generations an imitative Maple Leaf school of nature poetry followed in English Canada, but in French Canada in the 1890s occurred something of a "golden age" that culminated in the work of Émile Nelligan.

The modern movement in poetry began, in Smith's view, earlier in French than in English Canada. He indicates the way in which Paul Morin and René Chopin and his own group of McGill friends developed Canadian modernism. E. J. Pratt and Robert Choquette are seen as somewhat complementary poets in English and French Canada who wrote on large themes in long forms. Smith's account of the modern movement is interesting not only in itself but also for the light it throws upon what he and his friends were seeking to achieve in Canadian poetry:

The modern spirit in Canadian poetry has developed, as it has in Europe and the United States, in a progressive and orderly revolution. There was first a widening of the subject matter of poetry to include all aspects of contemporary life, especially the homely, the familiar, and the urban, treated realistically or with irony. At the same time there was a simplification of poetic language and an expansion of its scope to include the colloquial and the ordinary. This was part of the world-wide reaction against the rhetoric of the nineteenth century and academic doctrines of poetic diction. The free-verse movement in France and imagism in England and America were part of this technical revolution (17).

Smith considers the modern Canadian poets of importance to be writers like Earle Birney and Anne Hébert, Saint-Denys-Garneau and A. M. Klein. He concludes by suggesting that the Canadian poet can derive from his separateness and semi-isolation the advantage of "eclectic detachment," which, as he freely admits, "can be, and has been, a defect of timidity and mediocrity; but it can also be a virtue of intelligence and discrimination" (21).

"Eclectic detachment," which is presumably an aspect of identity in Canadian poetry, becomes the topic of his second essay. The Canadian poet can be eclectic in that he can pick and choose what he finds of interest and value and wishes to develop from the older English, French, and American traditions. He is "detached" from these traditions because of Canada's sovereignty and because of her attempt to develop an independent culture in North America. Smith quickly admits in his essay that "The effort to isolate a peculiar Canadian quality in the poetry of the Dominion has since Lighthall's time become a kind of occupational hazard of the Canadian critic and anthologist" (25).[2] The term "eclectic detachment," then, is really used in an attempt to define the Canadian poet's situation or cultural position. He notes that Northrop Frye has stressed the importance of an heroic, mythological, and narrative tradition as opposed to a lyrical one in Canadian poetry.[3]

Smith notes with concern the attacks upon nineteenth-century Canadian poetry that appeared in reviews of his *Oxford Book of Canadian Verse* (1960). He defends nineteenth-century Canadian poets on the grounds that "They simply show us what it felt like to live here in 1840 or 1860 or 1890." "Do we condemn the Bartlett prints," he asks, "because they are not like the paintings of the Group of Seven or later abstractionists?" (26). Finally, he considers the suggestion by the critic Milton Wilson[4] that it is because of the openness of Canadian culture that "eclectic detachment" becomes possible. Smith believes that Wilson "discovers in our very limitations the source of our special good luck" (29). Because of the brief tradition, Wilson argues, Canadians can draw from any time period in other traditions. "The Canadian poet," Smith quotes Wilson as saying, "has all the models in the language (not to mention other languages) at his disposal, but lacks the deadening awareness that he is competing with them" (29). Smith has only one reservation about Wilson's view and it reveals his critical judgement:

There is only one flaw, as I see it, in this provincial paradise. There is a serpent lurking in the phrase "lacks the deadening awareness that he is competing with them." It seems to suggest a double standard—which I am sure is far from Mr. Wilson's intention. The Canadian poet, like every poet, is in competition with every other poet, past and present, or more precisely, he knows he must be judged by as severe standards as any. And I believe that it is an informed freedom of choice that comes from being Canadian that has made it possible for our best poets to sustain this test—and perhaps more easily than if they had been English or American (29-30).

Smith's literary criticism is analytical, historical, and judicial. In the two "Synoptic" essays we do not see his analytic criticism in practice, but we do see his historical sense well displayed in his "Brief History of Canadian Poetry." He shows us the colonial, national, cosmopolitan development of Canadian poetry and reveals his critical discrimination in his selection of the best authors of that cultural evolution and achievement. Of the two essays in the "Synoptic" section, the first is, I think, the better. "Eclectic detachment" tells us something about the Canadian poet's cultural situation but is, finally, a red herring. Surely rather than worrying self-consciously about magpie borrowings from different languages and traditions it is now better for the Canadian poet to go ahead and write about human nature, nature, Canada, and the world. "A Brief History of Canadian Poetry," on the other hand, is an excellent introduction to Canadian poetry in English and French. Smith, in fact, possesses the ability he generously accords to Northrop Frye of being "able to see the always changing and always developing kaleidoscope of our literary history as a single pattern" (27).

II Before Confederation

The second section contains three essays concerned with Canadian literature before Confederation: "Colonialism and Nationalism in Canadian Poetry before Confederation," "Prose of the Colonial Period," and "The Canadian Poet to Confederation." Here Smith provides us with a deeper investigation into pre-Confederation Canadian literature.

In the first essay, the best and most original of the three, Smith argues convincingly that the backwoods poetry usually regarded as colonial poetry is, in fact, the truly national poetry of Canada, while the poetry that sought self-consciously to be nationalistic was the poetry that was most colonial. The Rev. E. H. Dewart, one of the first anthologists of Canadian poetry,[5] saw as early as 1864 the need in Canada for "the subtle but powerful cement of a patriotic

literature" (33). He realized too the stifling effect of a colonial habit
of mind and saw a developing conflict in Canadian culture between
independence and colonialism. As Smith puts it: ". . . colonialism
reveals itself most surely in the abstract and conventional patriotic
poetry, the ostensible subject of which might be devotion to the
Empire—or even to Canada—while true nationalism rises out of
the local realism of the pioneer" (34). The reason, for example,
why Charles Sangster (1822-93), hailed in his lifetime as Canada's
first national poet, failed to achieve that distinction was, in Smith's
view, because "he was not first a local poet" (36). The real source
of enthusiasm for Sangster, Smith believes, and the reason he was
hailed as a national bard, "was pride in the fact that here was a
poet who was *not* different from English poets but good enough to
be named in the same company with some of the most firmly
established of them" (37). At the end of the essay Smith does allow
that Sangster's poem "Brock" (1859) expresses a real sense of
national feeling eight years before Confederation. Sangster speaks
of "one voice, one people, one in heart / And soul, and feeling, and
desire!" (46) and expresses the unitary impulse that made Confederation possible.

However, as Smith quite rightly argues: "before this feeling
could find adequate expression, it had to be nourished in the very
earth of the new land. It is the pioneer realism and humour of the
backwoods poets that show the solid base of experience out of
which national pride and self-confidence alone could grow" (46).
Who were the backwoods poets who expressed their pioneer experience with the directness and realism that Smith so much admires? They were mid-nineteenth-century Scots-Canadian poets
like Alexander McLachlan, Alexander Glendinning, and Robert
Boyd whose work Smith rightly argues shows "Sincerity, simplicity, and directness" (40). Smith quotes a fine example of backwoods
humor and realism from Boyd's "The Bachelor in His Shanty."
Boyd, who came to Upper Canada from Ayrshire in 1830 and died
at Guelph in 1880 at the age of eighty-three, describes his "immi-
grant experience":

> To come to this strange land o' trees,
> The vile abode o' frogs and fleas
> Wi' no one near to sympatheese,
>   Or yet to hate us;
> Devour'd alive by slow degrees
>   By curs'd mosquitoes (40).

The formative influence on these poets was Robert Burns, and McLachlan was sometimes known as "the Burns of Canada."

The same argument that Smith advances about the poetry of the pre-Confederation period, he applies to the prose of the colonial period. Those who wrote self-consciously of nationality created a less truly national literature than those who wrote naturally and directly of their experience in Canada. The essay "Prose of the Colonial Period" was originally Smith's introduction to the first volume of his *Book of Canadian Prose (The Colonial Century)* (1965), whose purpose was:

to make available a representative selection of texts which illustrate the special character that geography, climate, and politics have imposed upon the sensibility and thought of the Canadian people. The inevitable, often unconscious, and sometimes artistic expression of this character in writing is what we mean by Canadian literature (47).

Here, unimpeded by elaborate theory, Smith tells us simply and directly what Canadian literature is.

He cites explorers and travellers like Samuel Hearne, Alexander Mackenzie, Alexander Henry, and David Thompson as the first un-self-conscious masters of Canadian prose: "These people created a literature simply by minding their own business and writing out of the immediate experience of the world around them and their struggle to master it" (47). He goes on to stress the practical nature of the literature of the colonial period (1763-1867): "At its best it has a native tang and a craftsmanlike goodness that more than compensates for any lack of polish or sophistication" (48). Alexander Henry's account of the Indian conquest of Fort Michilimackinac is, Smith feels, hard to equal, but better yet is Alexander Mackenzie's moving sentence that presents the completion of the first land crossing of Canada: "I now mixed up some vermilion in melted grease, and inscribed, in large characters, on the South-east face of the rock on which we had slept last night, this brief memorial: *Alexander Mackenzie, from Canada by land, the twenty-second of July, 1793*" (49).

For Smith, first-hand experience of place and time is superior to what he calls "painstakingly 'got-up' period pieces" (50). For this reason he prefers Mrs. Frances Brooke's *The History of Emily Montague* (1769) to later historical novels like William Kirby's *The Golden Dog* (1877) or Gilbert Parker's *The Seats of the Mighty*

(1896). At least she was there at the time and consequently her work "has a genuine social and historical interest" (50). Smith's discussion of prose of the colonial period concludes with a brief literary historical survey of such Canadian prose writers as the United Empire Loyalist Jacob Bailey, who excoriates his American "countrymen"; Dr. William Dunlop and Major John Richardson, who provide first-hand accounts of the War of 1812; Thomas Chandler Haliburton, whose Sam Slick sketches have led some to call him the father of American humor; and Joseph Howe, Haliburton's fellow Nova Scotian, who wrote proud and independent political defenses of the British North American colonies at the time of the Civil War in the United States. Smith speaks finally of the prose of the colonial period as "a literature of stress and tension" (54). He concludes:

The pull of opposing forces—from south of the border and from across the Atlantic—had to be resolved. And this was done not by opposing the one or submitting to the other but by utilizing both in order to attain, and then maintain, a balance. When that could be achieved, as it was with Confederation, the literature of colonialism ceased to have validity, and a new era, in letters as in life, opened before the Dominion (54).

The second essay (1965) seems less interesting and original than the first (1944), perhaps because twenty years later Smith's argument had become familiar. We have heard it before, and reiteration can blunt the force of a critical argument, even a good one.

The third and final essay is called "*The Canadian Poet* to Confederation." It first appeared in the journal *Canadian Literature* in 1968. How does it differ from the first essay in the section that had appeared twenty-four years earlier? At first glance not very much; as Smith admits in his "Author's Note," we may find when we consider the dates of composition of the essays "either a remarkable consistency or a remarkable lack of development" (xi). The first essay remains more original and stimulating than the third.

Yet when we read the third essay carefully, we find that Smith considers seven loosely related topics in Canadian poetry during the course of the essay. First, he discusses Northrop Frye's idea about the Canadian poet's tragic response to the terror of the Canadian landscape. What Smith thinks important is that the Canadian poet has fought the terror in the landscape. This is a good point, suggesting the stoicism and stubbornness present in both the Canadian character and Canadian literature at their best.

The second topic is the absence of a mythology in Canadian literature. Canada has often been seen as a country without a mythology. Confederation poets sought to import European and classical mythology into Canada, but except in a few cases (D. C. Scott, for example), only recently have Canadians connected themselves with the indigenous myths of the Indians. Smith wishes that this had happened earlier.

Third, Smith believes that the one myth that has attracted the Canadian poet is what he calls the myth of the machine. Quite early, Sangster saw the railway as an Iron Horse and E. J. Pratt showed concern with the machine throughout his poetry. Preoccupation with this, Smith believes, is the result of the importance of communications systems in a land as vast as Canada.

Closely related to this is the fourth theme, the difficult one of national unity. Once more it is pointed out that Sangster's "Brock" was written eight years before Confederation. National unity is a problem that has certainly beset the Canadian poet from before Confederation times to the present.

Fifth, Smith reverts to a topic, "colonial mindedness," that he had discussed in the first essay. But he proceeds to demonstrate in dealing with his sixth topic that "colonialism" had changed to "nationalism" to a quite considerable extent in the twenty-five year period between the publication of Dewart's *Selections from Canadian Poets* (1864) and Lighthall's *Songs of the Great Dominion* (1889). The quality of Canadian poetry had also improved. This Smith ascribes, rightly I think, to the genuine sense of national enthusiasm that Confederation had created. In 1889 there were simply more good poets in Canada than there had been in 1864. Lighthall could anthologize the work of Isabella Valancy Crawford and of men like Carman, Roberts, Lampman, Wilfred Campbell, and Duncan Campbell Scott, none of whom had begun to write when Dewart was gathering his poems together. The work of these writers is, Smith argues, "Canadian *poetry*" (59).

Seventh and last, Smith brings us up to date. He speaks of the two important changes that have taken place in Canada since the Second World War: the influx of European immigrants and the awakening of Quebec. This takes him back to the fourth problem, the problem of national unity, a dream that had unfortunately been dreamed by only half the Canadian nation. Smith's identification of the paradoxical operation of "colonialism" and "nationalism" is an important contribution to our understanding of Canadian literature.

III   *Poets of a Golden Age?*

The third section again contains three essays: "The Fredericton Poets," the brief "A Summing-up" about the Poets of Confederation, and "The Poetry of Duncan Campbell Scott," an essay in revaluation. The section continues Smith's analysis of the work of early Canadian poets.

The first essay (a Founders' Day Address delivered at the University of New Brunswick in 1946) concentrates upon the work of the two Fredericton poets of Confederation: Bliss Carman and Sir Charles G. D. Roberts. Acknowledging that they are both "classics" in the Canadian tradition, Smith feels that the time has come to submit their work to a closer critical scrutiny than it has yet received. In this way we will be able to sort the wheat from the chaff. Roberts, Smith finds, is at his best in his poems of country life and less successful in his patriotic and mystical verse. Carman's talent, he quite properly argues, is a very uneven one; his work is at its best when it is classically disciplined. And classical discipline is something that Smith finds in the background and education of the two poets. His essay is in part a tribute to Fredericton and to the University of New Brunswick, for he finds that Carman and Roberts both benefitted greatly from the fact that a Loyalist, Anglican, and classical culture had grown up in New Brunswick over a period of 100 years. Carman and Roberts, therefore, inherited a sense of continuity and tradition. Their schoolmaster, George Parkin, who had learned his Virgil at the plough, is singled out for special praise for imparting his love of the classics and of English poetry to his two pupils.

Smith begins his essay by showing the sense of tradition and vitality possessed by the original Loyalist settlers. They had their poets, men like Jonathan Odell, who had an instinctive sense of poetic craftsmanship. Odell was a direct inheritor of the satiric tradition of Dryden and Pope. Commenting on Odell's poem for George III's birthday of 1777, Smith remarks:

What cheerful high spirits and faith doomed never to be justified there was in this jolly poetry! And also (one who is interested in the craft of verse cannot help noticing) what a remarkable metrical skill is shown in the sudden surprising shift from the anapests of the first two lines of each stanza to the dactyls of the next two—a device that is repeated in the second half of each stanza. This was written by a man who had a good classical education, a clergyman of the Church of England, and the inheritor of a culture that the

Loyalists from New York, New Jersey, Pennsylvania, and the New England states were to bring with them into the Maritime provinces (66).

In his sensitivity to Odell's craftsmanship we are also made aware of Smith's. It is the continuity of this Loyalist-Anglican-classical tradition that concerns him. And he finds that it bore fruit in the 1870s and 1880s in the teaching of George Parkin and the poetry of Roberts and Carman, whose work Smith believes "is ready for the sort of trial by fire that would burn away the dross and leave the pure gold to shine all the more brightly, unmistakable and permanent" (67). Together with discriminating critical analysis, we have a sense of history. What the work of Carman and Roberts requires, Smith believes, is "a scholarly examination of the social and intellectual milieu out of which they have risen. And we must make a more rigorous effort to separate their best work from the larger body of their poetry which is less original, less intense, or less perfect" (67).

Exploring the classical education that Roberts and Carman received from Parkin, Smith notes the detail in which they analyzed passages of Virgil and comments that, perhaps, this "will help to refute those who think that a minute and searching analysis of a passage of poetry, whether it be by Virgil or Milton, deadens the feeling for what is truly poetic" (71). This is certainly a salutary reminder, and it shows Smith's critical thinking at its best. The tradition that Roberts and Carman imbibed in Fredericton is sensitively described as "calm, settled, and certain; conservative and no doubt rather narrow; a beautiful flowering of many traditions—the Loyalist, the Anglican, and the classical—all coming to terms with the wilderness after nearly a hundred years of struggle" (71). What this tradition allowed Carman and Roberts to create was what Smith calls "pure" poetry, "a poetry that is almost timeless and changeless, and that deals with the everlasting verities, human love, human loneliness, the sustaining strength of the earth, man's response to the voices, fancied or real, of nature" (72). This is the kind of poetry that Smith too has always stood for.

Smith, as noted, believes that Roberts's nature poems are superior to "his more ambitious mystical poems" (73). Roberts's poems of country life, Smith writes movingly, "are the distant fruit of the country boy, George Parkin, learning his Virgil as the horses paused for a moment turning at the end of the furrow" (73). As Wordsworth said to Coleridge at the end of *The Prelude:* "what we have loved, / Others will love; and we may teach them how." George Parkin

imparted his love of literature to Charles Roberts and it bore fruit in
Roberts's poetry.

Turning to Bliss Carman, Smith believes that "The first duty of the
critic who is anxious to rescue Carman's reputation from the reaction
that has followed a too-undiscriminating adulation is to define the
special excellence of Carman's best work" (73). This, he believes, is
the work that shows Carman's limiting vagueness and romantic
excess under the discipline of classical control. Parkin's enthusiasm
for Rossetti and Swinburne should not, of course, pass uncensured.
"The Fredericton Poets" is one of Smith's best critical essays. It
stresses the central importance of a real recognition of history and
tradition if cultural development is to be possible, and it reveals the
need to establish the poetic reputations of Carman and Roberts on a
proper basis by sorting their best from their inferior work. In fact, the
essay reveals the crucial and seminal part that tradition plays in the
creation of individual talents.

"A Summing-up," the second essay in the section, was first
published in 1942. In it Smith attempts to come to a judgement of the
work of the Confederation poets. He says that orthodox critical
opinion in Canada rates them highly. He does too, but he accepts
Professor James Cappon's reservation that Canada's best poets "have
devoted themselves too much to an almost abstract form of nature
poetry" (77).

Nevertheless, Smith wishes to stress that "their dependence upon
literary tradition is not a defect, for it went deeper than any mere
surface imitation. It arose out of a belief in the continuity of culture,
and in their best work it was a preserving and a civilizing force" (78).
Cultural continuity is naturally and rightly of central importance to
Smith's effort to give definition and shape to an authentic Canadian
tradition. The Confederation poets helped, by their sensitivity to
tradition, to create such a Canadian poetic tradition. Their theme,
Smith concludes, was "In general terms . . . nothing less than the
impingement of nature in Canada upon the human spirit" (78).

The third and final essay in section three, "The Poetry of Duncan
Campbell Scott," is best described as an essay in revaluation, first
published in 1959. In it Smith argues, wrongly I think, that Scott is
the best of the four Confederation poets. Some have argued for
Roberts's preeminence, but most, and I think rightly, accept
Lampman as the first of the Confederation poets.

Essentially Smith's argument is that Scott lived longer and produced more than Lampman. Scott also had a gift for narrative that

Lampman either lacked or did not live long enough to develop. Smith argues that Scott has greater diversity, appeals more fully to a modern taste, and attains universality more frequently than any of the other Confederation poets. To surpass him, Lampman (had he lived) would have had to broaden his scope, and achieve more variety and philosophic maturity than he had attained at the time of his death. In brief, Smith believes that "Duncan Campbell Scott stands first among the poets of his generation" (80). Admittedly, Scott's "At Gull Lake: August, 1810" is impressive and Lampman's "At the Long Sault" is not as good, but Lampman's nature poetry is better than Scott's, attaining a greater depth and perception. In short, Lampman's best poems are better than Scott's.

Smith sets out to discuss what he calls Scott's "metaphysic of love" and his "ambivalent attitude to nature and passion" (80). Smith asks:

Can we discover . . . the nature of the peculiar sensibility—and of the technical accomplishment that enables this sensibility to express and communicate itself; and then beyond that can we trace a line of development running through the whole body of Duncan Campbell Scott's work, and thus define and evaluate his contribution to our literature? (81).

These are good questions, but I'm not sure that the paper answers them any more than it convinces us finally of Scott's superiority to the other Confederation poets. Superior to Carman he certainly is, but it would be better to argue that he is equal to Roberts as a poet rather than superior to Lampman.

Smith shows us that Scott's poetry has musical qualities, that the *style* of his work is "unmistakably northern" (83). But I do not think that his work is equal to D. H. Lawrence's as Smith twice suggests. Smith tells us that "the characteristic virtue of Duncan Campbell Scott as an interpreter of nature and the real mark of his originality is the glowing fusion in his poetry of keenness of observation with clarity of thought so that the thing and the idea seem to be struck out together" (92). Smith shows us a number of Scott's virtues as a poet, but this essay is not as convincing in its central claims as the earlier essay on "The Fredericton Poets." A detailed discussion of Lampman is missing from this section of the book.

IV   *A Choice of Moderns*

The fourth and longest section contains seven essays; six of them concern individual modern Canadian poets and the section concludes

with a summing-up entitled "The Canadian Poet: After Confederation." The modern Canadian poets whom Smith considers are E. J.
Pratt, F. R. Scott, Earle Birney, Anne Wilkinson, Margaret Avison,
and P. K. Page. Certainly he chooses six of the best modern Canadian
poets for careful consideration, but we are entitled to feel that there
are some significant omissions. Just as the previous section "Poets of a
Golden Age?" would have been stronger had it included a detailed
discussion of Lampman, so "A Choice of Moderns" would have been
fuller and more definitive if it had contained essays on A. M. Klein,
Irving Layton, and James Reaney. However, let us consider the
choices that Smith has made.

Although not particularly well known outside Canada, E. J. Pratt
is, perhaps, Canada's most important poet; he could be called the
father of modern Canadian poetry in English. It is appropriate that
Smith should begin with a discussion of Pratt, acknowledging his
importance in these terms: "Pratt is the only Canadian poet who has
mastered the long poem or, to put it in a slightly different way, he is
the only Canadian poet whose world-view has been large enough to
compel forms of a large scale in order to express it" (114). In Canadian
poetry the long poem is of special importance; in it the vastness of
Canada can find expression. A heroic or epic form is necessary for
certain Canadian subjects, such as Brébeuf's life and martyrdom and
the building of the Canadian Pacific Railway. Pratt revealed in his
choice of subjects the importance of the historical poem in the
creation of Canadian culture.

Smith also finds Pratt important as a religious poet. Of Pratt, Smith
says, "What makes the problem of death so insistent and so intensely
felt for Pratt is his strong sense of life" (107), and we noted earlier how
paradoxical Smith's poetry is. Smith further notes in Pratt's poetry a
religious conflict and its resolution: "Most of his [Pratt's] poems, short
as well as long, have philosophical and religious overtones. They deal
with death and with man's struggle with Nature, and certainly some
are complex and difficult. They seem to lead up to an expression of
faith and then shy away from it" (112). Smith, however, acknowledges
that there are other poems where this is not the case. "But there are
poems that do make an affirmation of faith . . . and they are among
Pratt's finest poems. They mark a stage beyond 'The Toll of the Bells,'
'The Ice-Floes,' 'The *Titanic*,' and 'The Iron Door,' and they centre as
their climactic point upon the Rood and the sacrifice of Christ's
blood" (113). The essay could hardly be called definitive but it does

get to the center of Pratt's importance in Canadian poetry by stressing his achievement in longer forms and the religious nature of his work.

Smith moves in his next essay to a consideration of "F. R. Scott and Some of His Poems." Since Scott is one of Smith's closest friends and poetic and editorial associates in the modern movement in Canadian poetry, the essay is inevitably a tribute, but not an uncritical one. Smith considers Scott at his least successful when he is at his most didactic.

Scott's contribution to modern Canadian poetry was notable because "his energy, his generous goodwill, and the natural self-assertiveness that makes him an inevitable and stimulating leader were thrown into the battle for the new poetry in Canada as soon as it was joined in the mid-twenties" (115). Smith describes Scott's style as "exact, clear, and elegant"" (117). Interestingly enough, these are the very eighteenth-century qualities that also distinguish Smith's best work. Irony and satire, he continues, "are this poet's chosen weapons" (120). Certainly Smith is right; "W. L. M. K." and the earlier quoted "Canadian Authors Meet" are among Scott's finest poems. But there are also the northern lyrics such as "Lakeshore" and "Old Song" which like Smith's "The Lonely Land" discover and express "an austere cadence in the almost-silence of the northern wilderness" (119). Poems like these are what Smith calls Scott's "defining" poems (121), concerned with truth and "as well written as prose" (123). He concludes with an almost Johnsonian tribute to his friend:

In closing I should return to the personal. But actually I have not been away from it. The old dictum that the style is the man has never been more clearly illustrated than in the poetry of F. R. Scott. All his poems, from the gayest and lightest expression of delight in life, through his pointed and savage satires, to the profound lyrics I have been mainly considering, are informed and qualified by a sense of responsibility and an inescapable sincerity, which is serious but never solemn and rich without ostentation (124).

The close association between A. J. M. Smith and F. R. Scott has surely been one of the most productive friendships in the history of Canadian poetry.

In "Earle Birney: A Unified Personality," Smith argues that with Birney's publication of *David and Other Poems* in 1942, "it became apparent that a new poet had arrived, a poet who gave promise of being a worthy continuator of the tradition of heroic narrative established by Pratt and perhaps the precursor of a new school of modern poetry in Canada" (125). The second of these promises has been fulfilled rather than the first. Apart from "David," Birney has not really continued the Pratt tradition, yet he could certainly be called the father of West Coast Canadian poetry.

Smith is caustic about Birney's typographical experimentalism and says "paradoxically enough, his most successful experiment is the experiment of being traditional" (126). As with Scott, Smith thinks that Birney is at his least successful when at his most didactic. Smith speaks of "the futility of poetry as propaganda and . . . the corollary that action alone is adequate. This built-in demonstration of its own uselessness is what vitiates nearly all poetry that takes a bold stand against sin, and makes the social poetry of Birney, and of Frank Scott too, the weakest part of their work" (132). Smith, as we have seen, prefers what he has called "pure poetry."

Birney's success as a poet, Smith feels, lies in his creation of "a northern style, and an excellent one. Our sense of its validity is increased when we realize that it is not peculiar to Birney but is a common heritage" (130). Birney's subject Smith describes as "man's effort as microcosm to come to terms with society, nature, and the macrocosm in the brief moment of allotted time" (132). Perhaps what makes Birney, in Smith's view, "one of our major poets, perhaps since the death of E. J. Pratt our leading poet," (133) is his "orientation of himself and his place and his time in terms that are both emotionally and rationally satisfying" (131). Although Smith is right to choose Earle Birney as a leading modern Canadian poet, A. M. Klein, Irving Layton, or James Reaney could have been chosen for consideration with equal justice.

The section's fifth essay is "A Reading of Anne Wilkinson," Smith's introduction to the collected edition of Anne Wilkinson's poems. We can feel a special gratitude to Smith here, because in calling critical attention to Anne Wilkinson he is rescuing from neglect one of Canada's most unjustly underrated poets.

Smith isolates "the special qualities and peculiar virtues of Anne Wilkinson's poems" as "their being saturated . . . with light" (134). He feels that they reveal "a radiance of the mind, cast often on small, familiar things, or things overlooked before, and reflected back into the mind and heart" (134). Her poetry, Smith argues, benefits from its "traditional background" though "hers is the classic religion of Empedocles, Heraclitus, and Lucretius. What it celebrates is a metamorphosis" (136). Interestingly, at the heart of Smith's own poetry lies "metamorphosis" expressed through the idea of regeneration. One of Anne Wilkinson's central concerns, Smith suggests, is a "love-hate relationship with death" (138). "Love in the poetry of Anne Wilkinson," Smith writes, "is sometimes, as in 'Strangers,' a game of wit, but it is always also a sensuous involvement, not a twining of bodies and minds only but a mingling with the green sap of Nature in a wholly holy communion" (138). In Anne Wilkinson's poetry Smith also sees "an intense awareness, amounting almost to a foreknowledge, of death, and there is an air of faint desperation in the spells and magic rituals that are tried as exorcisms" (139). "Yet," Smith argues, "even in these final poems Anne Wilkinson was able to integrate the witness of all the senses into an affirming testimony of the beauty and richness of life" (141).

Smith believes that Anne Wilkinson's "work as a whole puts her, certainly, in the forefront of contemporary Canadian poets. She has helped us to be a little more aware and hence a little more civilized. Her poems are a legacy whose value can never be diminished" (141). This essay is one of the most original and important in Smith's selection of his critical essays. While he cannot be credited with discovering Anne Wilkinson's poetry, he can fairly be credited with recovering it from a critical neglect it suffers without him.

Smith is equally and rightly impressed with the poetry of Margaret Avison. Although her poetry is opaque and obscure at times, she is unquestionably one of Canada's finest modern poets. She has an added distinction among recent Canadian poets in refusing to overpublish her work. Her powers of selection and self-criticism are considerable. In "Critical Improvisations on Margaret Avison's *Winter Sun*," Smith invites us to "look at the words" (142) of Avison's poems. He finds her diction "as modern as it is archaic" (142). In Margaret Avison's poetry Smith finds that "the way things are seen and communicated is criticism (examination, interrogation, evaluation) as well as perception. The result is to transform perception into vision" (143). Of her humor he remarks that "Like the phoenix we carry the seed of a new birth within ourselves— humour is a sign of it . . ." (144). As we noticed in discussing Smith's poetry, the development of a sense of humor and self-irony is crucial to regeneration of character. Smith's concluding view of Avison is that she is one of the poets who reassociates or reintegrates Eliot's famous "dissociated sensibility." Smith's own efforts as both poet and critic are to recreate wholeness out of brokenness. He feels that Margaret Avison succeeds in this enterprise. His remarks proved prophetic, since his review of *Winter Sun* appeared in 1961, several years before Margaret Avison's Christian conversion. Smith writes: "rarely has a poet so compactly and richly identified sensation and thought. If there really *has* been a dissociation of sensibility, here we return magnificently to the old unity, and join with her among the guests at Bemerton who 'Did sit and eat' " (145). Smith's own work involves a pursuit of this "old unity" that he mentions here. George Herbert is the seventeenth-century poet with whom Smith seems to identify most fully in his Ph.D. thesis. Here he ascribes Herbert-like qualities to Margaret Avison that he also seeks in his own work.

Smith writes about the poetry of P. K. Page because, as he says:

No critic or literary historian . . . has made any serious attempt to deal at length with Miss Page's poetry or to define, illustrate, and evaluate her psychological symbolism and her strongly personal treatment of the universal themes of isolation and frustration—much less point to their transfiguration in certain epiphanies at the close of some of her most remarkable poems (147).

Smith finally places Page in a school of symbolist Canadian poets that includes Anne Wilkinson, Anne Hébert, Jay Macpherson, Daryl Hine, and Gwendolyn MacEwen. These poets "write not for the immediate moment alone. They are the poets who will live when the urbanized hitch-hiking social realists or the lung-born egoists of instant experience have been long forgotten" (155).

As with Avison's work, Smith finds P. K. Page's poetry to be a poetry of vision like some of the Metaphysical poetry of the seventeenth century. This is why he admires it; it has a quality he also seeks to express in his own work. To read Smith's literary criticism tells us a good deal about his poetry. This, of course, is because the criticism and the poetry are both parts of the same search for tradition and unity. He writes of P. K. Page: "Hers is in its final effect a poetry of vision, and it demands a quality of sympathy in the reader that its poetic richness helps to create. Indeed, to speak for myself, it casts a spell that has made it possible to value it not as vision only but as revelation" (148). Smith finds in P. K. Page's poetry "an affirmation of sincerity and of an integrity that is moral as well as aesthetic—a look at the worst as the images in so many poems of flowers and sun and summer are an attempt to find the best" (153).

In his concluding essay "The Canadian Poet: After Confederation," Smith notes that for the Canadian poet "the art that he must aim at is neither native nor cosmopolitan but universal" (163). If there is a division today in Canadian poetry, it is not between native and cosmopolitan schools, but between traditional and academic poets and those Smith calls the "new primitives" (162). It is poetry, Smith argues, "which expresses, indirectly and implicitly, the *spiritual reality* which makes a nation" (156). Thus, "creative maturity in poetry and the arts is the result of true nationhood" (160). Although Smith does not say so, Canada is still seeking this creative maturity as it is still seeking true nationhood. The Canadian poet after Confederation is a modern poet, and "The verse of the modern poet . . . tends to be critical and satiric. It is the flaws, shortcomings, and failures that the poet now sees looming large, while the ideal and the hope somehow fails to move him deeply enough for him to make poetry out of it" (156). Clearly the Canadian poet after Confederation, like poets everywhere, faces the bleak, universal problems of the modern world. He is distinguished by a special northern angle of vision that gives his work a "local habitation and a name."

V Some Polemics: Early & Late

Section five is the most important section of the book because it presents Smith's critical principles. He tells us what he thinks poetry and criticism are, and what they are about. This section should have been the first section of the book, but Smith presumably chose to give pride of place to the tradition of Canadian poetry.

The first essay in the section is called "Wanted—Canadian Criticism" and first appeared in the *Canadian Forum* in 1928. It is one of Smith's most important critical essays. In it he argues that "One looks in vain through Canadian books and journals for that critical enquiry into first principles which directs a new literature as tradition guides an old one" (167). Canadian writers enjoy a false popularity fostered by the Canadian Authors' Association. Here Smith attacks the "boosterism" of the Maple Leaf School whose chauvinism and parochialism had to be overturned before a modern movement that adhered to standards of international excellence could take root in Canada.

Smith asserted that "Without a body of critical opinion to hearten and direct them, Canadian writers are like a leaderless army" and continued: "It looks as though they will have to give up the attempt to create until they have formulated a critical system and secured its universal acceptance" (168). He then outlined the tasks that await Canadian criticism. First there must be freedom in the choice and treatment of literary subjects. Puritanism, Smith argued, had too strong a hold on Canadian culture. 1928 was the year in which *Lady Chatterley's Lover* was first published and Smith felt then that Canada needed to experience a work that was both successful and obscene. *Lady Chatterley's Lover* was not, of course, obscene. In Canada, Smith argued, realism is feared and irony not understood. Moral order was preferred to aesthetic harmony. The first of these arguments remains true, while the second has been hopelessly reversed today. Smith continues by asserting that Canada requires militant criticism that will establish standards and also philosophical criticism that will "examine the fundamental position of the artist in a new community" (169).

Canadian poetry, Smith suggests further, needs to acquire a deeper awareness of tradition. It still does; it is, in Smith's words, "altogether too self-conscious of its environment, of its position in space, and scarcely conscious at all of its position in time" (169). His conclusion is caustic and direct: "The heart is willing, but the head is weak. Modernity and tradition alike demand that the contemporary artist who survives adolescence shall be an intellectual. Sensibility is no longer enough, intelligence is also required. Even in Canada" (169). What is unfortunate is that Canadian criticism has failed to develop in the way that Smith set out for it here. Too many of the limitations in Canadian writing that Smith identified in 1928 persist in 1978 and are firmly enshrined as virtues. It will need stronger dynamite than Smith's to move them.

The second essay, "A Rejected Preface to *New Provinces*," was first published in *Canadian Literature* in 1965 although originally written to appear in *New Provinces* in 1936. It was not printed then because E. J. Pratt objected to it and F. R. Scott hastily supplied a replacement. On first reading the preface Pratt is supposed to have asked, "Who is this man Smith?"[6] Presumably Pratt objected to Smith's hostility to most earlier Canadian poetry. When he became an anthologist of Canadian poetry himself five years later, Smith also became kinder to Canadian poetry of the past than he was in 1936.

The essay *is* caustic and hostile to Canadian poetry, but there is truth in what Smith has to say. He writes:

The bulk of Canadian verse is romantic in conception and conventional in form. Its two great themes are nature and love—nature humanized, endowed with feeling, and made sentimental; love idealized, sanctified, and inflated. Its characteristic type is the lyric. Its rhythms are definite, mechanically correct, and obvious; its rhymes are commonplace (170).

Earlier anthologies of Canadian poetry such as those by W. W. Campbell (1913) and J. W. Garvin (1916) are attacked for the emotionalism and vagueness of their romanticism. "The fundamental criticism that must be brought against Canadian poetry as a whole," Smith says, "is that it ignores the intelligence. And as a result it is dead" (171). "Pure poetry" is what we should aim to create. He defines that as, "objective, impersonal, and in a sense timeless and absolute. It stands by itself, unconcerned with anything save its own existence" (172). The ivory towerism of the last sentence is surely to be deplored, though Smith's earlier requirements are worth seeking. By modern poetry Smith means imagism, a fusion of thought and feeling in the Metaphysical fashion described by Eliot and, if there is didacticism, a didacticism that is in the blood of the poem and is not just overt preaching. Poetry, Smith says, "is more concerned with expressing exact ideas than wishy-washy 'dreams' " (173).

Finally, Smith argues (and here he shows an awakened sensitivity to the Depression times in which he was writing), that the poet must end his isolation and establish a proper relationship to his society. Smith concludes "That the poet is not a dreamer, but a man of sense; that poetry is a discipline because it is an art; and that it is further a useful art: these are propositions which it is intended this volume shall suggest. We are not deceiving ourselves that it has proved them" (173). We can understand Pratt's reaction to this preface, but it was surely too cautious of him to object. Perhaps it was the objections of the publisher, Hugh Eayres, that weighed with him. Canadian poetry needed shaking up between 1900 and 1936 and, as a matter of fact, it still does. Canadian caution resists the polemical and limits itself by doing so.

Three years after the appearance of *New Provinces* in 1936 *without* his preface, Smith's article "Canadian Poetry—A Minority Report" appeared in the *University of Toronto Quarterly*. Here Smith argues that Canadian poetry needs a new anthologist, a task he undertook two years later. What is needed, he says, is "A revision, a weeding out, a new discovery—this is the task that is waiting for an anthologist with taste and courage. . . . What it is useful to know is not the historical significance of a poem in the development of Canadian literature but its absolute poetic vitality" (176). As he argues further, "Discrimination has never been an essential part of a Canadian anthologist's equipment" (177). To really achieve distinction Canadian poetry must forego its chauvinism and parochialism and face "open competition with the whole English-writing world" (178).

What Smith feels has limited Canada is a self-consciousness and also a kind of narcissism, "the rabid determination to find an elusive Canadianism in every bit of verse published in the Dominion. It is a determination that has distracted our critics for too long from the real problem of evaluation and has led them to judge the worth of poems not in terms of the whole range of English poetic experience but in terms only of Canadian things" (181). This produces a myopia and the whole malaise sounds like a prolonged adolescence.

An objective and uncompromising study of Canadian poetry *as poetry* remains to be written. Poetic excellence is taken for granted, or brushed aside as of only secondary importance, provided a piece of verse is an obvious manifestation of "the Canadian spirit." As a matter of fact, a sort of double standard has unconsciously been set up. Canadian poetry is treated as if it were produced in a vacuum. It is written by, for, and about Canadians, and it is evaluated solely in terms calculated not to wound Canadian susceptibilities (179).

Smith concludes the essay—which is, like "Wanted—Canadian Criticism," one of his best and most important—with advice to the Canadian poet: ". . . poetry does not permit the rejection of every aspect of the personality except intuition and sensibility. It must be written by the whole man. It is an intelligent activity, and it ought to compel the respect of the generality of intelligent men. If it is a good, it is a good in itself" (185). Smith's concern for wholeness here is characteristic; he sets out to wean Canadian poetry away from the Maple Leaf romanticism which had been its chief affliction in the early years of the century. By stressing the importance of thought and intelligence in the poetic process, he attempts to direct Canadian poets towards the reassociation of sensibility that Eliot had set as the goal of modern poetry.

In his essay "Poet," first published in 1956, Smith sets out to define poetry and the function of the poet. He describes poetry as "the application of emotion to ideas" (188). He ascribes the poet's unpopularity to his being too critical of modern society: "He is the one, . . . who tells on us, the teller of unpleasant truths, the secret conscience of society, the revealer of unconscious guilt. No wonder he is derided, exiled, driven into the wilderness, and made a scapegoat" (188). The poet must be true to nature and to human nature. "He must cultivate in himself accuracy and clarity; he must identify himself with things and men's feelings about things" (188-89). Poetry, Smith states, performs both useful and essential functions. He calls it "an instrument of self-awareness" and quotes R. G. Collingwood to the effect that art is "the community's medicine for the worst disease of mind, the corruption of consciousness" (189). Poetry is finally described as "language that refuses to make compromises" (190). With this in view, Smith tells us that "A poem is a work of art—a thing made; and the first responsibility of the poet is to see that it is well made—made as well as he can make it" (191).

The penultimate essay in the volume appeared in 1965; "A Survey of English-Canadian Letters—A Review." It is a review of the first edition of Carl F. Klinck's *Literary History of Canada*. The importance of the essay lies in Smith's defense of critical evaluation. Taking exception to Northrop Frye's view that evaluation is only "an incidental by-product" of literary criticism, Smith stresses that "evaluation *is* the end, purpose, and *raison d'être* of criticism" (203). The *Literary History of Canada* fails, as Smith says, because it is only the rare contributor who can "go beyond description and become not simply a recorder but a critic whose ultimate task is evaluation and whose essential method is *literary analysis*" (201). What the *Literary History of Canada* leaves undone and what is now needed is "a comprehensive 'critical history' by a single author who can combine scholarly research with imaginative interpretation and who has enough faith in the literary quality of the best work drawn from all kinds of writing—science, history, travel, biography, and autobiography as well as poetry and fiction—to make evaluation his first business" (205). Smith's review says a number of things that need to be heard in the bland, uncritical circles of Canadian literary commentary.

The final essay consists of Smith's "Impromptu Remarks Spoken at the International Poetry Conference, Man and His World" at Montreal's Centennial Year Exposition, "Expo 67." Smith's essential humanism becomes immediately clear. He describes poetry as "a human activity" and says "that if it is to be fully relevant, it must speak for the whole man, the whole human being" (206). The poet is concerned with "an effort to integrate personality" (207). For this reason, poetry is described as "not an artificial hallucinatory drug; it is an instrument of search and research" (207). Smith continues by saying, "I would like a poetry that avoids the loud, the general, the abstract, a poetry that is music for the inner ear" (207). He then concludes by asking and answering a question: "What good is this quiet intellectual poetry in the age that we live in, this violent wicked age of crises? Well, such poetry nourishes the human soul and encourages, it seems to me, whatever in man is strength to resist tyranny, cruelty and indifference, either in the state or in himself" (207). Smith is clearly a humanist who sees poetry as essential to both individual and cultural wholeness.

VI   *A Personal Epilogue*

Towards a View of Canadian Letters ends with two essays: "A Self-Review" and "The Poetic Process: On the Making of Poems." The book thus follows Eliot's idea of tradition and the individual talent; the first four sections are devoted to discussion of the Canadian poetic tradition, the last two to Smith's critical principles and his reflections on his own poetry and the craft of verse.

"When I write a poem I try to know what I am doing—at least with respect to craft" (211), Smith writes in "A Self-Review." Speaking of his *Collected Poems* (1962) he observes that "Some people may think it presumptuous to call a book of only a hundred short, mainly lyrical pieces of verse *Collected Poems*—but actually that is exactly what it is" (211). Unlike a number of modern and contemporary Canadian poets, Smith has been scrupulous about what he has published. The high standards of literary excellence he has advocated as a literary critic he has, in most cases, applied to his creative practice. Further, in his poetry he has sought unity and believes that his poems, however different, possess an "under-lying unity" (213). "I do not believe in progress in the ordinary sense of the word. The more recent poems in this collection are neither 'better' nor 'worse' than the earlier," (213) Smith states, and shows that like his criticism his poetry has either "a remark-able consistency or a remarkable lack of development" (xi). This is why the chronological or developmental view is not particularly appropriate in Smith's case. It is true that like most poets he improves poems, such as "The Lonely Land,"[7] through different drafts, but at root his work as poet, critic, and anthologist has a central and unifying impulse to advance and describe the Canadian tradition.

As a traditionalist he seeks what Eliot calls "impersonality." "My poems," Smith writes "are not autobiographical, subjective, or personal in the obvious and perhaps superficial sense" (213). He is also attracted to Christian and Platonic ideas (216), though he remains (in his poetry, at least) something of an uncertain Christian. Finally, as a traditionalist, he finds himself naturally opposed to "the confusion of values in the modern world of political propaganda, mass media brainwashing, and cold-war bilge" (216). Smith's self-review reveals his respect for tradition and his innate conservatism.

"The Poetic Process: On the Making of Poems" begins with a critique of psychoanalytical criticism: ". . . if the poem produced is not more interesting than the account of *how* it was produced, one would be hard put to it to write a defense of poetry" (217). The poet may not wholly understand the sources from which his poems come but once he has a first, "inspired" draft on paper he has the craftsman's responsibility to see that his work is well made. Smith reveals further that he does not mind the unpopular appellation "academic poet," so long as it suggests a poet who is aware of tradition and has a sense of art and craftsmanship. He finds too an advantage for the poet in being a university teacher: "In the experience of other poets in other times he has a series of touchstones that help him understand and evaluate his own practice" (218). Again he expresses an unpopular view, yet again he is right: a university is surely an ideal place for a poet since it allows him time to read and teach the work of other poets.

Why does the poet write? Smith suggests that fame and relief from pain are two powerful motives. He quotes Paul Valéry's "Propos sur la poésie" on the subject of creation:

The poet awakes within a man at an unexpected event, an outward or an inward incident: a tree, a face, a "subject," an emotion, a word. Sometimes it is the will to expression that starts the game, a need to translate what one feels; another time, on the contrary, it is an element of form, the outline of an expression which seeks its origin, seeks a meaning within the space of my mind. . . . Note this possible duality in ways of getting started: either something wants to express itself, or some means of expression wants to be used (219).

In a discussion of his own poem "The Archer," Smith admits his long-standing preoccupation with death. Over the years he says he has achieved "acceptance by the intellect (though not necessarily by the will) of the idea of death" (226). What has preoccupied him in a number of his poems is, he believes, "the guilty knowledge hidden in the unconscious self of the identity of love and death" (227). Despite this personal recognition, the poet seeks to make impersonal, objective, and universal his subjective experience. Again Smith takes his cue from Eliot: "For Eliot, and for the modern poet generally, poetry is not an expression but a distillation of experience; passion is transmuted; and suffering (if a physiological or medical term may be permitted) is digested" (230).

In conclusion, it is striking that Smith closes the selection of his critical essays with the quotation from Santayana that he uses as the epigraph to his poems. This further establishes the interdependence between his critical and poetic work. "Every animal has his festive and ceremonious moments, when he poses, or plumes himself, or thinks; sometimes he even sings and flies aloft in a sort of ecstasy," says Santayana. Smith's poetic art is dedicated to joy, his criticism to a comprehension of the nature of poetic joy. His critical work gathered in *Towards a View of Canadian Letters* deserves a place of distinction in contemporary Canadian critical writing. Considered beside Northrop Frye's *The Bush Garden*, D. G. Jones's *Butterfly on Rock*, and Margaret Atwood's *Survival*, critically, it is the best of the four, for it is the only one of them that is centrally concerned with making critical judgements which is, after all, what literary criticism is about.

CHAPTER 4

The Anthologist

I *Introductory*

A large part of A. J. M. Smith's literary career has been devoted to his work as an anthologist, particularly of Canadian literature. In anthologies of Canadian poetry, criticism, and prose he has tried to select examples of the best Canadian writing and thereby define and give shape to a developing Canadian tradition. Indeed, one of the central concerns of his career has been to contribute to and help create a Canadian literary tradition. Thus, to consider Smith's work as an anthologist is to examine once again the central intention of his literary career.

Of course, Smith has anthologized other works than works of Canadian literature. Indeed, he describes himself in a recent essay, which provides the best guide to his work in this area, as "a compulsive anthologist."[1] He began to compile lists of books and then lists of the best books even as a child. "I saw nothing ridiculous," he tells us, "in Palgrave's astonishing attempt, as he confessed it in the Introduction to *The Golden Treasury*, 'to include . . . *all the best* original Lyrical pieces and Songs in our language . . . by writers not living—*and none beside the best*.' "[2] His first serious work as an anthologist was an anthology of modern Canadian poetry, *New Provinces*, which he edited with F. R. Scott and which was published in 1936. As argued earlier, this anthology was of crucial importance in establishing modern poetry in Canada.

Smith's next work as an anthologist was in some ways his most important. In 1941 he received a Guggenheim Fellowship to prepare an anthology of Canadian poetry to replace such outdated works as W. W. Campbell's *Oxford Book of Canadian Poetry* (1913) or J. W. Garvin's *Canadian Poets* (1916). Smith's *The Book of Canadian Poetry* was published in 1943, went into a second edition in 1948, and a third in 1957. It led Smith to examine in detail the history and development of his country's poetry and to select and organize into an integrated anthology the best examples of it. Two years after the appearance of *The Book of Canadian Poetry* Smith received a Rockefeller Fellowship to prepare an anthology of Canadian prose. But where *The Book of Canadian Poetry* took two years to make, *The Book of Canadian Prose* took twenty. The first volume, later called *The Colonial Century*, appeared in 1965 and the second, *The Canadian Century*, not until 1973.

In the years between 1945 and 1965 a veritable stream of anthologies by Smith appeared. In 1947, for example, he published what has become a very popular college anthology, *Seven Centuries of Verse: English and American*, which received a second edition in 1957, and a third in 1967. This was followed four years later, in 1951, by *The Worldly Muse: An Anthology of Serious Light Verse*, which is now something of a collector's item since most of the copies of the book were destroyed in a warehouse fire.[3] This anthology helped Smith prepare the ground for his next anthology of Canadian poetry *The Blasted Pine* (1957), which, like *New Provinces* twenty years earlier, he edited with F. R. Scott. *The Blasted Pine*, subtitled *An Anthology of Satire, Invective and Disrespectful Verse*, breathed a refreshing breath of satiric north wind into the atmosphere of Canadian literary discussion. It received a second edition in 1967.

Before *The Blasted Pine*, another college text-anthology, *Exploring Poetry*, edited with M. L. Rosenthal, appeared in 1955 and went into a second edition in 1973. The culmination of Smith's work as an anthologist of Canadian poetry, though, appeared in 1960. Forty-seven years after W. W. Campbell's *Oxford Book of Canadian Verse*, A. J. M. Smith's *Oxford Book of Canadian Verse* appeared. It was a truly Canadian anthology since one-third of the poems were in French. Seven years later, in Confederation year, Oxford University Press published his anthology of *Modern Canadian Verse*, once again in English and French. By 1960, then, A. J. M. Smith had emerged as probably the most important anthologist of Canadian poetry we have yet seen. His anthologies of Canadian poetry are as important for his generation as W. W. Campbell's, W. D. Lighthall's, or E. H. Dewart's earlier anthologies had been for their generations of Canadians. And although Smith did not emerge as an anthologist of Canadian prose until 1965, in 1961 and 1962 respectively he edited and published two anthologies of

Canadian criticism: *Masks of Fiction* and *Masks of Poetry*. One final piece of work as an anthologist was his *Essays for College Writing* which appeared in 1965.

In this chapter, we will first consider his work as an anthologist of Canadian poetry by examining selected examples in this area: *The Book of Canadian Poetry, The Blasted Pine*, and finally *The Oxford Book of Canadian Verse*. Then, after discussing *Masks of Fiction* and *Masks of Poetry*, we will conclude with an examination of his *Book of Canadian Prose: The Colonial Century* and *The Canadian Century*. In this way we should be able to gain a fair estimate of A. J. M. Smith's work as a literary anthologist.

II The Poetry

New Provinces was simultaneously Smith's first large contribution to Canadian poetry as a poet and his first enterprise as an anthologist of Canadian poetry. It was designed to call attention to modern poetry in Canada. It attempted to redirect Canadian poetry and though little bought and read when it appeared it has gained an historical significance in "the making of Modern poetry in Canada."[4] It was a "group" anthology since it contained work by the Montreal poets Leo Kennedy, A. M. Klein, F. R. Scott, and Smith himself, but it also contained selections of poems by the Toronto poets Robert Finch and E. J. Pratt. Seeking to be controversial, the anthology created controversy even among its contributors, since (as we have seen) Pratt objected to Smith's preface.[5]

Smith's reflection on *New Provinces* is as follows:

I can see that the book could have been just that much better and more useful had we broadened even more the scope of our interest, and included some poems of Eustace Ross and Raymond Knister. Earle Birney's first poems in the *Canadian Forum*, of which he became literary editor in 1936, were just too late for us, but we ought to have taken something from Dorothy Livesay's *Signpost* of 1931. Then instead of the rather indifferent shorter poems of E. J. Pratt, how much stronger the book would have been had we persuaded him to let us use *The Cachalot*, his first masterpiece! (*CCA*, 6).

In defense of Smith's earlier decisions, it takes time to achieve representativeness; he sees Canadian poetry, even modern Canadian poetry, differently in 1976 than he did in 1936. The point about *New Provinces* is that the book as it appeared in 1936 was necessary and that it helped to establish, albeit belatedly, a modern poetry movement in Canada.

What is of more interest when we read "Confessions of a Compulsive Anthologist" is to see how Smith is now prepared to view some of the judgements of Canadian poetry that he expressed in 1936 as arrogant and hasty. Why did Pratt object to Smith's preface? Smith writes in 1976:

> The objections to some of it were valid enough. Worse than the rejection of all Canadian poetry before ours—or at least that to be found in the anthologies of Garvin and Campbell—was the tone of rather youthful arrogance and perhaps the scornful epigrammatic style—faults (and virtues) to be found also in my 1928 *Canadian Forum* article, "Wanted—Canadian Criticism" (*CCA*, 5).

The parenthetical "and virtues" is good: the seventy-four-year-old Smith is not prepared to take back everything that the thirty-four-year-old had said, and he is right not to do so. He still believes quite rightly that the "rejected" preface would have had a salutary effect had it been published in the 1930s. However, in discussing his preparations for *The Book of Canadian Poetry* of 1943 Smith admits that his dismissal of Canadian poetry in 1936 was not made from a very solid base of knowledge of Canadian poetry:

> Then, sometime in 1939 or '40 I received an invitation to apply for a Guggenheim Fellowship—Frank Scott, my good angel, I think, had suggested my name. Casting about for a suitable research project it occurred to me that as I knew practically nothing about the historical development of a genuine Canadian poetry it would be a service both to myself and possibly my country to seek out the same and try to illustrate its characteristics from the point of view of a modern sensibility (*CCA*, 6).

This is precisely what Smith seeks to achieve in *The Book of Canadian Poetry*. He tries to show us "the historical development of a genuine Canadian poetry" which means in essence that he seeks to show us the Canadian poetic tradition. By "genuine" he seems to mean poems that are both *Canadian* and *poetry*. The illustration of characteristics that Smith refers to probably involves his notorious division of Canadian poets into "native" and "cosmopolitan" schools. As mentioned earlier, Smith came to accept Northrop Frye's suggestion that the "native" / "cosmopolitan" division, rather than dividing Canadian poets rigidly into schools, exists in the mind of each Canadian poet. Better still, we might say that the Canadian poet achieves universality and wholeness as he expresses the native and the cosmopolitan, as he finds the universal features in Canadian experience. Further, what Smith's creation of an anthology of Canadian poetry "from the point of view of a modern sensibility" meant was that W. W. Campbell's *Oxford Book of Canadian Verse* (1913) had to be brought up to date and an illustration given in *The Book of Canadian Poetry* of what had happened to Canadian poetry in the years from 1913 to 1942. The latter in brief was the arrival of the *New Provinces* and other modern Canadian poets. Smith also sought to reduce Campbell's emphasis upon the Confederation poets, Roberts, Carman, Lampman, D. C. Scott, and Campbell himself. Beyond this he set out to take a closer look at the late eighteenth- and earlier nineteenth-century roots of Canadian poetry in English. What were the results of his enquiry?

He begins with a section of "Indian poetry and French-Canadian Folk Songs," what we could call the pre-English roots of Canadian poetry. This is not original, since Lighthall does the same in *Songs of the Great Dominion* (1889), but he is right to include material of this kind. In fact, it becomes increasingly apparent that a truly "Canadian" anthology of Canadian poetry would not only include French-Canadian material, as Smith realized by the time of his Oxford book (1960), but also Eskimo and Indian material, together with poems written in the "unofficial" languages of Canada such as those found in English translation in such a volume as *Volvox* published by the Sono Nis press in 1971.

The second part of *The Book of Canadian Poetry* is called "Pioneer and Emigrant: The Rise Of A Native Tradition." Smith, in my judgement, does not quite take the English roots of Canadian poetry back far enough. Instead of beginning with selections from Oliver Goldsmith Jr.'s *The Rising Village*, he ought to have begun with something of Jonathan Odell's. Odell, the Loyalist Tory satirist, provides us with the kind of link with the English past that we need in order properly to perceive the difference between the United States and British North America.

After Odell, Goldsmith allows us to follow "the rise of a native tradition," which describes the Canadian landscape in traditional English and Scottish forms in the work of Joseph Howe, Alexander McLachlan ("the Canadian Burns"), Charles Sangster ("Canada's

first national bard"), and Charles Mair. A trio of Charleses is
completed by the poet in the section who has sparked the greatest
controversy, Charles Heavysege, who has been vigorously praised
and derided both by Canadian critics and by critics outside
Canada. Nathaniel Hawthorne and Coventry Patmore both
acclaimed his closet drama *Saul* when it first appeared in 1857,
yet critics reviewing Smith's *Book of Canadian Poetry* disagreed
sharply over his achievement which Smith himself, in retrospect,
feels he overrated. Smith was later to make further distinctions
among the pioneer and emigrant poets whose work created a
native tradition and see in the work of McLachlan and fellow
Scots-Canadian poets like Glendinning and Boyd, who unfortunately were not anthologized in 1943, the true makers of a national
poetry while some of the poets who aped cosmopolitan traditions
or sought self-consciously to build a national poetry proved themselves to be the real colonials. Sangster, for example, is found by
Smith to be neither local nor national enough.[6]

Smith calls Part III "The New Nationalism: 'The Golden Age.' "
He sees the coming to maturity of Canadian poetry in the work of
Isabella Valancy Crawford. Though his argument for "maturity" at
this point is premature, we can nevertheless agree with Smith that
in Isabella Valancy Crawford's work we have one of the first
instances of a poetry that *is* truly Canadian—that is northern and
western rather than American or British, that treats Canada in a
new and Canadian way. Like Emily Carr later, Isabella Valancy
Crawford creates an Indian animism that brings a new, authentic,
and original life to Canadian poetry. This is particularly evident in
poems of hers like "The Canoe" and "Malcolm's Katie." Of course,
there is evidence of Tennyson and Swinburne there too; in fact,
the balance between imitation or influence and originality is finely
drawn. But what is freshly and uniquely Canadian in Crawford is
her unique response to the Canadian landscape that required new
descriptive methods and resulted in a real, because truly experi-
enced, sense of place.

If Crawford is the "native," George Frederick Cameron (1854-
85) is the "cosmopolitan" poet. In the first *Book of Canadian
Poetry* they are balanced and paired, though Crawford is surely the
more interesting of the two. She, more than Cameron, prepares
the ground for the first real flowering of Canadian poetry in the
work of the Confederation poets. In selecting the work of these
poets (who, Smith admits, might well be the best group of Cana-

dian poets to have appeared), Smith's task is one of discriminating selection rather than uncritical inclusion of the kind we find, for example, in Campbell's *Oxford Book*. Smith has argued elsewhere that we have failed so far to sort the wheat from the chaff in the case of poets like Roberts and Carman. In the first *Book of Canadian Poetry*, Smith's selection from the Poets of Confederation is parsimonious but just. He includes only their best work and does not jumble good Carman with bad as Campbell and Garvin had done. In Smith's anthology we begin to see the thew and sinew of Canadian poetry in English. We begin to think of Roberts, Lampman, Campbell, Carman, and D. C. Scott in terms of "The Mowing," "Heat," "How One Winter Came In the Lake Region," "Low Tide on Grand Pré," and "At Gull Lake"; in terms, in short, of their best poems.

Part IV is perhaps more an act of duty than an act of love. This is the period between 1900 and 1925 which Smith calls "Varieties of Romantic Sensibility" and against which he reacted as a young modernist. The poets of the Maple Leaf School are here represented. Smith keeps the selection lean and yet is generous to them, though there is nothing of Wilson Macdonald's. Tom MacInnes and Robert W. Service are included as are, at another pole, Francis Sherman and Marjorie Pickthall, so that we move from the hairy-chested to the refined and the religiose. The best poem in the section is also Canada's best-known poem, John McCrae's "In Flanders Fields."

The final two parts are devoted to "Modern Poetry," which Smith divides into "The Native Tradition" and "The Cosmopolitan Tradition." In subsequent editions this division is dropped. John Sutherland, unfairly, suggested that Smith's distinction was intended to be qualitative[7] and that Smith was implying that the native tradition was inferior. More helpfully, Northrop Frye has suggested that rather than there being two traditions Canadian poets are divided or oscillate between "native" and "cosmopolitan" poetic impulses.[8] Smith has accepted Frye's suggestion while pointing out that in both cases what any Canadian poet worth his salt seeks is universality. There is some point, though, in trying to determine what Smith meant by the division in 1943. It seems, in essence, that the poets of "the native tradition" are placed there because they write about Canada, in particular, though not entirely, about the Canadian landscape, while the "cosmopolitan" poets are concerned with more general themes. The division is probably as simple as that, and Smith, in fact, has observed its presence from the beginning of Canadian poetry in English. There have always been those poets who have written about Canada and those who have written on general themes. Many, perhaps most, Canadian poets have done both and Smith's most perceptive observation in this general connection is that native poets, like the early Scots-Canadians, produced a more truly *Canadian* poetry than those poets who self-consciously wrote patriotic poems.[9] Put simply, Sir Charles G. D. Roberts' sonnet "The Potato Harvest" is a more Canadian poem than his patriotic Confederation piece "Canada," in part at least because it is a better poem.

It would be hard to argue that the poets of "The Cosmopolitan Tradition" are better than their "Native Tradition" brothers. They simply write about different things. *The Book of Canadian Poetry* concludes with a very helpful bibliography of "Special Collections in Canadian Libraries," "Anthologies of Canadian Poetry," "Canadian Literature," "Studies of Individual Authors," and "Historical and Cultural Background." Dewart's anthology of Canadian poetry of 1864 is historically the most important, and W. D. Lighthall's *Songs of the Great Dominion* (1889) is nationally the most important, but *The Book of Canadian Poetry*, when it appeared in 1943, became the best anthology of Canadian poetry in English.

Smith, as noted earlier, has not simply been an anthologist of Canadian poetry. *Seven Centuries of Verse* is an anthology of English and American verse and his anthology of "serious light verse," *The Worldly Muse,* is drawn from poetry in English from Chaucer and Skelton to Auden and the Canadian poet L. A. Mackay. Smith's anthologies of English verse inevitably fertilize and support his work as an anthologist of Canadian verse. As Smith himself observes, "*The Worldly Muse,* however, did serve me in good stead when, three or four years later, I began working on a second collaboration with Frank Scott that was to result in the publication of *The Blasted Pine: An Anthology of Satire, Invective, and Disrespectful Verse Chiefly by Canadian Writers*" (*CCA*, 11). *The Blasted Pine* is an important anthology of Canadian poetry primarily because it is satirical. Satire is a neglected though necessary art in Canada, which needs poems that "are sharply critical, in one way or another, of some aspect of Canadian life that has more often been accepted uncritically."[10] In their introduction, Scott and Smith wrote:

All satire, indeed, and most invective, is moral: it asserts or implies a standard of value. It makes judgements, and demands or seizes the right of self-assertion. It takes sides, speaks out, and enters actively into social, political, or moral engagements. It is a form of action, and its writers are partisans. They are very much needed in Canada today—and to-morrow (p.xvi).

The most memorable poet of the anthology is the too much neglected Canadian satirist L. A. Mackay. His "And Spoil the Child" (1931) may be Popeian pastiche, but it is very good Popeian pastiche:

> See first where gentle Gallus gushes forth
> Hymning the happy springtime of the North,
> The sparkling drifts, or else the flaming trees,
> In twenty thousand lines as like as peas.
> How languidly the liquid lyrics loll
> And dangle off into a dying fall,
> And smooth as celluloid, or pulp-wood silk,
> As toothsome and sustaining as skim milk.
> While Swinburne, tumbling with unquiet breast,
> Mutters, "I'm dead; for God's sake let me rest!"[11]

The way in which the word "dead" in the last line cuts two ways and satirises both Swinburne and his Canadian imitator is an instance of satiric language at its best. In the same vein F. R. Scott's "The Canadian Authors Meet" is surely the anthology's best, most famous, and most representative single poem. Appearing first in 1957, *The Blasted Pine* was revised and enlarged in 1967 for Centennial year as an appropriate tribute. Scott and Smith remark in their "Note to Revised Edition":

The time has come . . . to bring our blastings up to date . . . and to fire another salvo in the long war of wit against complacency, a warfare that has not become any the less urgent in this year of centennial celebration (p. xix).

The Oxford Book of Canadian Verse in English and French, which is the apex of Smith's achievement as an anthologist of Canadian poetry, is both a refinement and culmination of the work begun for the original *Book of Canadian Poetry*. It is also a new departure because of Smith's inclusion of his carefully selected French material. Good taste, Smith has frequently argued, is one of the anthologist's prime requirements, and he shows good taste and good sense in his balanced selection of English and French poems. This is at last, for almost the first time, a truly *Canadian* anthology.

In "Confessions of a Compulsive Anthologist," Smith speaks at some length of the origins and making of this anthology:

As long ago as 1942 in a survey of Canadian anthologies published in the *University of Toronto Quarterly* I had castigated the puerilities of Wilfred Campbell's *Oxford Book of Canadian Verse* of 1913. . . . At the end of the discussion of the 1913 *Oxford Book* I had written, "A revision is badly needed." It was not until the fifties were drawing to a close that this became a possibility. I began pestering my friends Ivon Owen and William Toye, who were then in editorial command at the Canadian Oxford Press, to let me try and, rather to my surprise, they succeeded in persuading the Delegates of the Press in England to do just that. I think it was perhaps my suggestion that the book should include an ample selection of French-Canadian poetry in French that turned the trick (*CCA*, 12).

Smith's selection of Canadian poems in English involved a further refinement of the work undertaken in the three editions of *The Book of Canadian Poetry*, while his selection of French-Canadian poems was a wholly new venture:

I read first the old standard comprehensive *Anthologie des Poètes Canadiens* of 1920 by Jules Fournier and the modern *Anthologie de la Poésie Candienne Francaise* of Guy Sylvestre, with whom I corresponded and who gave me the benefit of his critical acumen. I bought the collected poems of Fréchette, Nelligan, Des Rochers, Choquette, and Saint-Denys-Garneau, and the various volumes of Alain Grandbois, Anne Hébert, and the younger poets of Hexagon and *Parti Pris*. I read these—or perhaps I should say read *in* them—aided occasionally by a dictionary and sometimes by my old friend and master-translator John Glassco. I also sought out all available English translations, particularly those of Gael Turnbull and, of course, Frank Scott. The results seem to have been successful, and there were few if any complaints, either about the proportions—one-third of the poems included were in French—or the choices themselves (*CCA*, 12).

His reading of French-Canadian poetry indicates a remarkably similar parallel development between poetry in the two languages of Canada. The first important poetry in French-Canada was a nationalist, patriotic poetry; "a national historian, François-Xavier Garneau, and a national poet, Octave Crémazie, gave an impetus to French-Canadian patriotism at the very moment it had become essential to survival. The national pride of the defeated and, as they felt, abandoned colonists of New France was stimulated and their wounds to some extent salved by the glowing pages of Garneau and the impassioned verse of Crémazie" (*Oxford Book of Canadian Verse*, p. xxxi; hereinafter abbreviated as *OBCV*).

Crémazie's successor, Louis Fréchette, Smith notes, was the first Canadian poet to achieve international recognition: "His poems published in Canada and in Paris during the late seventies were crowned by the French Academy, and it seemed at last as if something done in the North American dominion was meritorious enough to place beside the masterpieces of the old world. Fréchette acquired enormous prestige among his countrymen—English as well as French" (*OBCV*, p. xxxiii). Fréchette "was winning recognition outside the narrow confines of his own province at the very moment that English-speaking poets in the Maritimes and Ontario—Roberts, Carman, Lampman, and Duncan Campbell Scott—were about to achieve something of the same sort of success in London and Boston" (*OBCV*, p. xxxiii). The Confederation poets were primarily nature poets and their work is paralleled in French-Canada to some extent by the *terroir* poets Pamphile Le May, William Chapman, and Nérée Beauchemin who wrote a sober, realistic poetry about *habitant* life and the land.

Canadian poetry in English attained maturity and enjoyed a kind of golden age in the 1890s; so too, as Smith tells us, did French-Canadian poetry. In 1895 the *Ecole Littéraire de Montréal* was established and among its members there was a turning away from patriotic towards a more cosmopolitan poetry. Such poets as Jean Charbonneau, Paul de Martigny, Gonzalve Désaulniers, Charles Gill, Charles Dantin, Albert Lozeau, and Émile Nelligan "were inspired in their experiments with form and in their more emotional and original themes by the various poetic movements in France, particularly Parnassianism and Symbolism" (*OBVC*, p. xl).

Like the Scots poet William Soutar, Albert Lozeau was an invalid who was confined to his bed with a form of spinal paralysis from the age of eighteen. Smith tells us that Lozeau became a "poet of the closed-in life. With great elegance, charm, and modesty—'Je suis resté neuf ans les pieds à la hauteur de la tête,' he wrote once, 'cela m'a enseigné l'humilité'—he developed a narrow but pure talent for the inner life of sensibility and reverie, which provided him with material for three volumes of verse between 1907 and 1916" (*OBCV*, p. xl). But the most vibrant personality of the group was Émile Nelligan, subject of a haunting painting by the French-Canadian painter Lemieux. Nelligan was a Chatterton or Rimbaud-like figure "whose work," Smith tells us, "was done before he reached twenty. In 1899 his mind collapsed, and though he did not die until 1941 he remained hopelessly insane, one of the most tragic figures in the history of North American letters" (*OBCV*, p. xli). Smith, of course, has translated Nelligan's famous "Le Vaisseau d'or."

The modern movement, Smith argues, began earlier in French-Canada than it did in English-Canada. Smith offers the plausible explanation that this is because the modern movement in the arts began earlier in France than it did in England. Paul Morin, one of the chief French-Canadian modernists, held a place in French-Canadian poetry somewhat similar to Smith's place in the poetry of English-Canada. Smith speaks of Morin in terms of "the perfection of his forms and the dedicated spirit of his devotion to art" (*OBCV*, p. xlii). This kind of comparison is admittedly somewhat dubious, but if Smith could be argued to have a counterpart in Paul Morin, the only French-Canadian poet who seems, at all, to resemble E. J. Pratt is Robert Choquette:

who was born in 1905 and who launched his first volume *A travers les vents* in 1925 when Pratt was producing his earliest original work. Choquette repudiated the aestheticism of Nelligan and the exoticism of Paul Morin and cultivated instead, not a poetry of the soil or the village but a universal and emotional poetry that was to be at once national and filled with energy and thought (*OBCV*, p. xliv).

It would be hard to find equivalents in English-Canadian poetry to the important French-Canadian poets Saint-Denys-Garneau (1916-43) and his cousin Anne Hébert. It would probably be more useful to look instead to French-Canadian painting to the career of Paul-Émile Borduas to find an equivalent to the tragic career of Garneau. Other modern and contemporary French-Canadian poets to be anthologized by Smith are Pierre Trottier, Alain Grandbois, François Hertel, Gilles Hénault, Roland Giguère, and Jean-Guy Pilon. These modernists were followed by a group of radical and revolutionary poets who find their way into Smith's later anthology *Modern Canadian Verse in English and French*. Until recently the paths of English and French Canadian poetry have been remarkably close. In both cases we find patriotic, landscape, and modernist poetic movements and even in contemporary, radical poetry we might notice similarities, though the targets of each

group are different. French-Canadian radical poets seek separation
from English-Canada while their English-Canadian brothers seek
release from the cultural domination of the United States. Both, as
Margaret Atwood would argue, seek survival. Thus a kind of parallelism continues; differences of language do not override a common
humanity, and though the experience of English- and French-
Canadians in northern North America has been different, it has
also had its common features. Together with the more important
fact that Canada is one nation, this is what makes Smith's *Oxford
Book of Canadian Verse in English and French* such an important
volume, helping to give Canadians a sense of cultural unity. This,
presumably, is one of the reasons why Smith found such pleasure
in a particular French-Canadian response to his *Modern Canadian
Verse*. He writes:

> The Canadian and American reviews of the modern book were good,
> but the one which pleased me most was a French one by the Montreal
> critic Jean Ethier-Blais in *Le Devoir*. While, like many of his compatriots,
> Blais did not quite approve of pairing off English and French poems in
> the same volume, he wrote most generously of the French selections,
> "Qui a guidé Professeur Smith dans son choix des oeuvres de langue
> française? Personne, semble-t-il, sinon lui-même. Pour ma part, je trouve
> ce choix parfait. . . ." What more could an anthologist ask? (*CCA*, 13).

We can see, then, that Smith has wide experience as an anthologist of poetry, having published seven separate anthologies of
verse, most of which he has seen through two, and sometimes
three, editions. Anthologizing, it should be clear by this point, is a
form of literary criticism. In Smith's view:

> every critic, and certainly every anthologist, should examine his own
> position in relation to every poet he is concerned with. I want to know
> whether I have discovered the principles that guide me inductively by the
> examination and analysis of many poems or whether I have made certain
> assumptions and then found poems to sustain them. I hope the former
> (*CCA*, 13).

How does Smith go about making one of his anthologies? "In
working on an anthology my practice has always been to read as
many poems as possible and to choose those that strike me as most
appropriate to the purpose in hand—to illustrate in the Canadian

collections the variety and growth of poetry in Canada" (CCA, 13). In discussing how the organizing principles of an anthology are determined Smith continues:

But the nature of that variety and the stages of its growth—these will be lefined and determined by the consideration of the poems. Perhaps this is to tackle two ends of the problem at once, but it works. This process, when fruitful, begins with a sudden flash of recognition, a sudden onrush of pleasure—the emotional sources of critical insights are sometimes as significant as those of poetry (CCA, 13).

This is an important passage because it shows how closely Smith's activities as poet, literary critic, and anthologist are related. Smith discovers the "Canadian" or "native" in the lines of Roberts' "Ice" when, "The water shrank, and shuddered, / and stood still—," or in "The Mowing" where, "The crying knives glide on; / the green swath lies." These lines create for Smith a feeling similar to that expressed by Lampman on observing a field of dead mulleins in November:

> And shuddering between cold and heat,
> Drew my thoughts closer, like a cloak,
> While something in my blood awoke,
> A nameless and unnatural cheer,—
> A pleasure secret and austere (CCA, 13).

What is so "Canadian" or "native" about a field of dead mulleins, we might well ask? It is certainly not such a flattering image of Canada as the maple leaf or the beaver, but what it expresses in Smith's view is a peculiarly Canadian feeling "of the special ardours and grandeurs of our northern environment" (CCA, 14). And the expression of a sense of the north, its desolation and its strength, is as Smith rightly realizes a defining characteristic of Canadian poetry.

Smith also observes innocence, simplicity, and *naïveté* in Canadian poetry "that instinctively avoids rhetoric and metaphor alike—a characteristic I would rather call *modesty* than *timidity*" (CCA, 14). He concludes by describing this quality as "a sort of graceful diffidence" (CCA, 14). We can certainly see this quality in Smith's poetry, in, for example, a poem like "Epitaph," and it is also present in his work as an anthologist and as a literary critic.

Before examining Smith's work as an anthologist of criticism of

Canadian literature and of Canadian prose, we should, perhaps, consider his description of "the ideal anthologist":

> The ideal anthologist is a paragon of tact and learning. In him an impeccable taste is combined with a completeness and accuracy of information that is colossal. To an understanding of social development and social upheavals he adds a sensitiveness to the finest nuances of poetic feeling. He is unprejudiced, impersonal, humble, self-confident, catholic, fastidious, original, traditional, adventurous, sympathetic, and ruthless. He has no axe to grind. He fears mediocrity and the verses of his friends. He does not exist (*CCA*, 14).

The whole is self-irony like the poem "My Lost Youth," yet it is clear that the qualities indicated here are equally necessary to the poet and the literary critic. With "graceful diffidence" Smith denies that he is himself such an "ideal anthologist," yet it is fair to say that he comes as close to being an "ideal anthologist" of Canadian poetry as anyone yet.

III *The Criticism*

Smith's anthologies of critical essays on Canadian literature *Masks of Fiction* and *Masks of Poetry* appeared in 1961 and 1962 respectively. Each anthology is organized differently being determined in each case by Smith's sense of tradition. Smith does not believe that a coherent tradition of Canadian fiction has yet emerged; however, he does believe that a tradition of Canadian poetry already exists.

Because Smith believed then that there was not yet a discernible tradition in Canadian fiction, the critical essays about it require a greater degree of organization, presumably in the interests of fostering the development of such a tradition. Thus, he divides his anthology of critical essays on Canadian fiction into three sections. In the first section, "The Writer Himself," he places three essays about the writing of fiction by three Canadian novelists, Frederick Philip Grove, Ethel Wilson, and Hugh MacLennan. The section begins with Grove's "In Search of Myself," followed by Wilson's "A Cat Among the Falcons," and MacLennan's "The Story of a Novel." In this way Smith seeks to set the problem of writing fiction in Canada before his reader in a compelling way by presenting examples of personal testimony from actual practitioners of the art.

Since the development of a tradition depends inevitably upon respect for the past, the second section of *Masks of Fiction*, called "A Backward Glance," contains essays concerned with some of the best examples of Canadian prose of the past. The section begins with E. K. Brown's essay "The Problem of a Canadian Literature." The "problem" for a colonial literature, in Brown's view, is colonial-mindedness, by which he means the slavish imitation of models from the imperial center, and the failure of authors to develop a fresh and original response to their new country. His essay is followed by V. L. O. Chittick's "The Gen-u-ine Yankee," which is about the Nova Scotian Tory satirist Thomas Chandler Haliburton, the creator of "Sam Slick" and one of the fathers of "American humour." Haliburton is unquestionably the father of Canadian comic prose, if we can be allowed to speak of a pre-Confederation author as "Canadian." Although he does not write novels (his "Sam Slick" pieces are comic-satiric sketches), he is nevertheless one of the finest nineteenth-century Canadian prose writers. As Smith clearly understands, good comic prose is better than the many bad novels published in Canada in the nineteenth century. These slight, sentimental, or turgid romances are, of course, the reason for the absence of a real tradition of Canadian fiction.

The third essay in the section is E. A. McCourt's "Roughing It with the Moodies." Once again Smith chooses to present a discussion of Canadian prose of good quality. Only by emulating the best writing of the past will Canada develop the fictional tradition it desires. The fourth and final essay in the section is by the contemporary Canadian comic novelist Robertson Davies and concerns the Canadian comic sketch-writer Stephen Leacock. We can, perhaps, understand the idea of tradition that Smith seeks to develop if we consider that the influence of Haliburton on Leacock was creative and that both in turn have had a beneficial influence upon Robertson Davies's comic novels. We might even be able to detect the emergence of a tradition of Canadian comic fiction from the sketches of Haliburton and Leacock to the comic novels of Davies. Smith's selection of material points us in the direction of conclusions of this kind.

Masks of Fiction concludes with a third section of five essays devoted to five modern Canadian novels or novelists. The section is called "Here And Now" and contains F. W. Watt's "Morley Callaghan as Thinker," George Woodcock's "A Nation's Odyssey," about the novels of Hugh MacLennan, William McConnell's "Recollections of Malcolm Lowry," M. W. Steinberg's "A Twentieth-Century Pentateuch," about the poet A. M. Klein's single novel *The Second Scroll*, and finally Hugo McPherson's "The Mask of Satire," about the novels of Robertson Davies. Smith's anthology is thus designed to assist in the creation and development of a tradition of Canadian fiction by carefully selecting for our attention discussions of the best Canadian fiction and prose.

In his "Introduction" to the essays Smith quotes as "a characteristic example of the sobriety and modesty that true criticism must never relinquish" (*Masks of Fiction*, p. vii; hereinafter abbreviated as *MF*), Claude Bissell's assessment of Canadian fiction from the *University of Toronto Quarterly* of 1954. Although we might feel with some justice that Canadian fiction has improved in the twenty years since that date, Bissell's words still provide a salutary reminder. After all, a Canadian has yet to win the Nobel prize for literature which means, presumably, that it has yet to produce a Saul Bellow (though he *was* born in Canada) or a Patrick White. Bissell writes:

It would, I think, be generally acknowledged that the best Canadian prose is not to be found in our fiction. This negative tradition was firmly established in the nineteenth century. Whatever their merits as romancers, Richardson and Kirby wrote abominably. Even Mrs. Moodie, who could muster a good sturdy prose in her autobiographical volume, became pompous and stilted in her fiction. Poets like Heavysege, Campbell, and Roberts, who had their moments of lucidity and directness in verse, fell into a decline when they turned to fiction. The line of bad fictional prose has not been broken in this century. Even a superior novelist like Grove wrote so awkwardly that it is doubtful whether he ever managed to communicate his artistic vision. The inflated style favoured by the nineteenth century novelists has largely disappeared, but it has given way to conscientious flatness and a humdrum realism which are often just as unattractive. There are shining exceptions each year, but the characteristic is so general that it can be made the key to an analysis of our fiction (*MF*, p. viii).

Smith rightly feels that Bissell has presented the truth here (a rare and welcome phenomenon in Canadian criticism, though his judgement of Roberts's prose is surely too hard), and argues that we have to capitalize upon our "shining exceptions." This is why Smith focusses attention upon Morley Callaghan, Hugh MacLennan, Ethel Wilson, and Robertson Davies. In 1961 they were

Canada's four best novelists, though none of them could be re-garded as classic. Smith writes, "All four are distinguished not only for the bulk and seriousness of their work but for the significance of their subject-matter and the adequacy of their interpretation of experience. Furthermore, they have all won a certain amount of recognition and sympathetic attention in the United States and England. Their appeal is more than local or national" (*MF*, p. viii).

During the course of the "Introduction" Smith has occasion to define what he means by an "academic critic." His definition throws light upon his own criticism since he has tried to live up to this definition. "The term 'academic critic' is not intended to suggest pedantry, stuffiness, or dullness. On the contrary, it im-plies solidity, learning, intelligence, and wit" (*MF*, p. viii). Smith argues that this kind of criticism should concern itself with the "few best" works of Canadian fiction of the past and with the modern Canadian novels that show an improvement upon the works of the past. He includes in the volume essays on Malcolm Lowry's *Under the Volcano* and A. M. Klein's *The Second Scroll*, works that he describes as "isolated masterpieces" that "approach greatness." He, also, mentions the recent arrival of "such varied, excellent, and serious novels as *The Mountain and the Valley*, *The Sacrifice*, *The Apprenticeship of Duddy Kravitz*, *The Rich Man*, *Tay John*, *Execution*, *The Double Hook*, and *The Luck of Ginger Coffey*" (*MF*, p. ix), some of which merit Smith's praise and some of which do not.

When we turn to the past, Smith suggests, we discover "that the best work has been done on the periphery of the novel." This is an insight that Smith follows up to advantage later in his *Book of Canadian Prose*. The humorous sketches of Haliburton, the pioneer narratives of Mrs. Moodie, and the animal stories of Roberts are all superior, in Smith's view, to the novels of Richardson, Kirby, and Sir Gilbert Parker. "Indeed," Smith argues "it is not in fiction but in poetry that the progress of Canadian letters from colonial times to the present is most clearly marked. The earlier novelists were less adventurous and on the whole less successful than the poets" (*MF*, p. ix). This is an old chestnut that critics of Canadian literature love to roast. Edmund Wilson, for example, in his book *O Canada* argues the reverse, though I think that Smith is right. As Smith says, "Except for Haliburton there is no one until we come to Leacock and Grove able fully to engage the capabilities of our best and liveliest critics. Consequently it is not the *growth* of the novel in Canada but the variety of theme and execution in the best work of our chief contemporaries that is illustrated here" (*MF*, p. ix). Smith is wrong to pass over Sara Jeanette Duncan's *The Imperialist* (1904), yet we may agree with the main thrust of his argument that in the poetry "growth" is detectable, and therefore a sense of tradition. In Canadian fiction, Smith suggests, this is not the case. Once again we can see that to be an anthologist is to be a literary critic, since critical judgement is central to the creation of any good anthology. Smith concludes his "Introduction" with an explanation and justification of his selections for inclusion in the book.

When we turn from *Masks of Fiction* to its companion volume *Masks of Poetry* that appeared a year later we find that the essays are simply arranged chronologically rather than topically. This is because Canadian poetry has, in Smith's estimation, a coherent tradition. Interestingly enough, the twelve essays in the volume are divided equally between nineteenth- and twentieth-century Canadian poetry in English.

The volume begins with the introductions to the two most important anthologies of nineteenth-century Canadian poetry in English. First we have the Rev. Edward Hartley Dewart's "Introductory Essay" to his *Selections from Canadian Poets* (1864) followed by W. D. Lighthall's "Introduction" to his *Songs of the Great Dominion* (1889). Smith thus begins his anthology of critical essays about Canadian poetry with the introductions of two earlier anthologists. Again we see that the anthologist is responsible for helping to form tradition and for providing insights into the works that he chooses to anthologize. Dewart's and Lighthall's introductions are followed by Archibald Lampman's "Two Canadian Poets: A Lecture, 1891," a selection from James Cappon's *Roberts and the Influence of his Time* (1905), and L. A. Mackay's "Bliss Carman: A Dialogue." Thus, in the first five essays in the volume the chief concern is with nineteenth-century poetry.

In the middle of the volume are two essays of more general interest, a selection from W. E. Collin's "Natural Landscape" and W. P. Wilgar's "Poetry and the Divided Mind in Canada." The nineteenth-century selection is then balanced by five essays on twentieth-century Canadian poetry, so that even though the volume is less obviously designed than *Masks of Fiction*, its organization still shows symmetry and pattern. Smith has said that his favorite poet is Alexander Pope,[12] and it seems that even an

anthology of critical essays by Smith will possess a Pope-like balance. In his selection of essays on twentieth-century poetry we
have Earle Birney's "E. J. Pratt and His Critics," Northrop Frye's
"Letters in Canada: Poetry, 1952-1960," James Reaney's "The
Canadian Poet's Predicament," Milton Wilson's *Other Canadians
and After*," and Irving Layton's "Foreword to *A Red Carpet for the
Sun.*"

In his "Introduction" to the volume Smith states simply that
Masks of Poetry is intended to provide "a representative sampling
of critical and expository writing on Canadian poetry by Canadian
scholars and men of letters from before Confederation to the
present time" (*Masks of Poetry*, p. vii; hereinafter abbreviated as
MP). The volume, Smith continues, "is limited by being representative and, it is hoped, by being representative of the best" (*MP*, p.
vii). The concern of the essays is "the impact of poetry on the
culture and society of Canada" (*MP*, p. vii). They are presented
chronologically in order to reveal "changing motivations and developing values," in short, to provide us with an insight into not
only the "literary condition" in Canada but also into the tradition of
Canadian poetry. As Smith says: "This should make it possible for
the general reader as well as the student to appreciate the inevitable differences between good writing of the past and good writing
of the present—and, what is even more important, to recognize
their underlying and abiding similarity" (*MP*, p. vii). Therefore,
the poetry of nineteenth-century Canada is neither dismissed nor
patronized. Smith tells us further that "no extravagant claims" are
made "for the native product." The essays "are all based on the
reasonable and intelligent assumption that we have the right, or
rather the obligation, to take the productions of our own culture
seriously and to examine them in the light of general principles"
(*MP*, p. viii). He then repeats his contention that "It is in poetry,
much more than in fiction, that progress in Canadian letters has
been most clearly and uninterruptedly marked," and speaks about
the relationship between "political unity and literary maturity"
(*MP*, p. viii).

Concluding his "Introduction," four years before the publication
of Carl F. Klinck's *Literary History of Canada*, Smith apologizes
for the fact that "The present collection of essays, I am afraid, will
emphasize—and this may not be the least of its services—the lack
of any single unified but comprehensive survey of our literature.

We have never had one that was really adequate" (*MP*, p. x). Smith's anthologies of Canadian poetry, criticism, and prose with their critical introductions, in fact, attempt to supply this need. Indeed, in the final paragraph, Smith writes:

> Of the essays included here, there are enough and they are of sufficient variety to suggest most of the questions that confront the writer in Canada. While the emphasis is as it must be on contemporary writers, the dozen or so poets who have demonstrated beyond any doubt that Canadian literature has come of age, there is also enough material from the past or about the past to give the enquiring reader some understanding of how the present condition came about. If this can be achieved these essays will have served one of the main purposes that moved the editor to bring them together. (*MP*, p. xi).

Once again we can see that Smith's central intention as an anthologist is to define a Canadian literary tradition. Any careful examination of his literary career reveals immediately his deep concern for the cultural development of his country. Smith also reveals in his work a true reverence for tradition. He is a conservative who wishes to conserve the human achievements of the past so that they will direct, modify, and inspire the works of the present. As an anthologist of literary critical essays on Canadian literature, Smith once more reveals himself to be a literary critic of genuine discrimination, tact, and good taste.

IV The Prose

A. J. M. Smith's two-volume *Book of Canadian Prose*, as has been noted, was twenty years in the making. Smith recently commented:

> After the success of the Canadian poetry anthology it seemed only natural to begin a study of our prose literature, and in 1945 I was given a Rockefeller grant for two years to travel in Canada and begin such a study. This time I met and talked chiefly with novelists. I have very happy memories of the kindness I received from Theodore Roberts in Digby, Nova Scotia, Morley Callaghan, whom I already knew, in Toronto, W. O. Mitchell in High River, Alberta, and Ethel Wilson, Malcolm Lowry, and Howard O'Hagan, my old Editor-in-Chief from the *McGill Daily* days, in Vancouver. You will see how hard I worked on this project, as Stephen Leacock might have put it, when you realize that the first volume of *The Book of Canadian Prose*, now retitled *The Colonial Century*, did not

appear until 1965, twenty years after, and the much larger second volume, *The Canadian Century*, until 1973. But such procrastination was actually all to the good. The book was able to include selections from the writers of the explosive fifties and sixties—material well worth waiting for (*CCA*, 11).

It is interesting again to note that Smith speaks of his work as an anthologist of Canadian prose as a "study." Indeed, it is a critical study and selection of prose from colonial times to the present.

The chief importance of the "study" lies in the serious attention given to nonfictional prose. Some of the best Canadian prose is to be found in travellers' accounts of their journeys, in comic sketches, in political speeches, and in studies, for example, of Canadian history. As examples we could cite Smith's selections from Samuel Hearne's *A Journey from Prince of Wales's Fort in Hudson's Bay, to the Northern Ocean . . . in the Years 1769-1772* or from Alexander Mackenzie's *Voyages from Montreal . . . through the Continent of North America to the Frozen and Pacific Oceans in 1789 and 1793*. The selections from Susanna Moodie's *Roughing it in the Bush*, concerned with a slightly later period, are also impressive pieces of good writing. As Smith says of the writing of this early period in his "Introduction":

The characteristic literature of the colonial period is practical and utilitarian. It is the knowledgeable product of men and women whose main business is not letters as a profession or writing as a fine art. Their writing is an instrument or a tool to be used in the main task of subduing the wilderness, achieving an emotional adjustment to the new environment, and securing their kind of social or political organization. At its best it has a native tang and a craftsmanlike goodness that more than compensates for any lack of polish or sophistication. This applies especially to the work of the fur-traders and explorers in the north and west. Samuel Hearne, Alexander Henry, and David Thompson write with a steady downright competence akin to the skill with which they used the sextant or wielded the paddle. These are the writers of our heroic age, as are the Jesuit missionaries of that of our French-Canadian brothers. They found, each in his own way, a style, rough and ready though it often was, which was commensurate with the great story they had to tell, or rather the great work they had to do (*The Colonial Century*, pp. xiv-xv; hereinafter referred to as *CC*).

The key phrase here is surely "achieving an emotional adjustment to the new environment" which is the central concern of so much Canadian literature both early and late.

The volume also includes selections from Thomas Chandler Ialiburton's *Clockmaker* sketches of Sam Slick, in which we can ee the beginnings of Canadian comic writing. Haliburton was presumably the first Canadian author to gain an international reputation, since the Sam Slick sketches were well known in the United States and Britain as well as in the Canadas, and Sam Slick was for a time as famous as Charles Dickens's Sam Weller. It concludes with such important political documents as Joseph Howe's *Open Letter to Lord John Russell* and Sir John A. Macdonald's speech about Confederation made in the Legislative Assembly, Quebec on February 6, 1865. Throughout Smith's purpose is to present examples of the best prose from British North America during the colonial, pre-Confederation period. The selections from Frances Brooke's *The History of Emily Montague*, the first North American novel, are, in fact, the only selections in the volume from a work that is formally a work of fiction.

In his "Preface" to the volume Smith indicates that:

The prose literature illustrated in this panorama of almost exactly a hundred years of Canadian history forms a companion to the poetry in the earliest section of *The Book of Canadian Poetry*. The two books together will provide the reader with a broad picture of the literature of our colonial period. On the whole, the writing in the present book differs from the verse of the same period and from most of the later literature. It is more practical, more purely expository, usually simpler, and generally less sophisticated and literary. This is sometimes a defect or a limitation, but more often it is not. Directness, homeliness, and an absence of self-consciousness can give the comparative artlessness of primitive or colonial writing the virtues of strength and simplicity.

Directness, strength, and simplicity are qualities that any literature departs from at its peril. These qualities, as Smith shows in his selection, are there at the root of Canadian literature.

Smith, finally, defines the prose of *The Colonial Century* as:

a literature of stress and tension. The pull of opposing forces—from south of the border and from across the Atlantic—had to be resolved. And this was done not by opposing the one or submitting to the other but by utilizing both in order to attain, and then maintain, a balance. When that

could be achieved, as it was with Confederation, the literature of colonialism ceased to have validity, and a new era, in letters as in life, opened
before the Dominion (*CC*, p. xxii).

As if to confirm this sense of separate regions moving finally into
unity the volume is presented in five sections, the first four of
which contain examples of prose from different parts of colonial
Canada: "Lower Canada and the Maritimes in the Eighteenth
Century," "Explorers and Fur-traders in the North and West,"
"Pioneer and Colonist in Upper Canada," and "Two Nova Scotian
Masters." Appropriately the unifying Part V is called "Fathers of
Confederation." *The Colonial Century* is yet another example of
Smith's unifying work as an anthologist. He seeks, indeed, to show
in the volume how Canadian unity was achieved, just as his *Oxford
Book of Verse in English and French* is a work designed, in part at
least, to sustain Canadian unity. His literary career has been a
patriotic act in many respects, a career of loyalty to his country.

  The Canadian Century is appropriately twice as thick a volume
as *The Colonial Century*. There has been much more prose written
in Canada during her second century and it would not be unrea-
sonable to assume that there has been twice as much good writing
in that time. The volume is divided into two parts that have three
and four sections respectively. Part I is called "The Expanding
Dominion, 1867-1914" and its three sections are "Affirmation and
Conflict," "Local Color, Sentiment, and Satire," and "Essays and
Belles-Lettres." Section one contains a selection from a political
speech by Edward Blake, parts of Louis Riel's defence speech, and
Sir Wilfrid Laurier's speech on Riel's execution. It concludes with
a selection from Goldwin Smith's *Canada and the Canadian Ques-
tion* (1891) in which he advocates Canadian union with the United
States.

  "Local Color, Sentiment, and Satire" reveals the stirrings of a
fictional tradition in Canada. Sir Charles G. D. Roberts's animal
story "The Watchers in the Swamp" (1922) represents "local
color," though surely Roberts's animal stories are something more
than that. Sentiment is evident in Ralph Connor's *Glengarry
Schooldays* (1902) which presents very well a schoolboy drama of
loyalty in a Scots-Canadian community. For satire we have a
selection from Sara Jeanette Duncan's *The Imperialist* (1904),
perhaps the best of Canada's earlier novels, and finally three
selections from Stephen Leacock's work.

There are three examples of essays and belles-lettres in section three. First we have Robina and Kathleen Lizars's account of "Tiger" Dunlop (whose account of the War of 1812 appeared in *The Colonial Century*) from their *In the Days of the Canada Company* (1896). This is followed by Duncan Campbell Scott's "The Last of the Indian Treaties" (1906) and Tom MacInnes's "Chinook Jargon" (1926), both of which provide us with insights into Indian life in Canada.

The second part of *The Canadian Century* is an anthology of twentieth-century Canadian prose, divided into four sections: "Interpretations of Politics and Culture," "The Rise of Critical Realism," "Character and Comedy," and "Toward Symbolic Narrative." The first section includes selections from some of Canada's best historical writing. Among the authors represented here are Arthur M. Lower, Frank Underhill, Donald G. Creighton, E. K. Brown, Marshall McLuhan, Northrop Frye, George Woodcock, and Ramsay Cook. The final three sections are devoted to selections from different kinds of Canadian fiction. In section two, for example, we are given examples of realism from the writing of Frederick Philip Grove in the 1920s through the work of Morley Callaghan, Hugh MacLennan, Sinclair Ross, Hugh Garner, and Hugh Hood to the present. We might reasonably ask why a writer like Mavis Gallant is omitted, though even the best anthologies cannot include everyone of merit. "Character and Comedy" allows us to see that Haliburton and Leacock did not write in vain, for from them has developed a minor tradition that includes writers like Ethel Wilson, John Glassco, Robertson Davies, W. O. Mitchell, Jack Ludwig, Mordecai Richler, and Alice Munro. Most of these writers are also, of course, realists since "character" is emphasized here as well as "comedy."

The final section of Part III is devoted to selections from fiction of a more experimental or symbolic kind. Here we have work by Howard O'Hagan, A. M. Klein, Malcolm Lowry, George Whalley, Sheila Watson, Margaret Laurence, Leonard Cohen, and Dave Godfrey.

The large question that Smith concerns himself with at the end of his "Introduction" to *The Canadian Century* is:

. . .whether the survey of English-Canadian prose literature since Confederation can tell us anything about the much discussed and sometimes tedious question of Canadian identity. Do we find here, for instance, a unity, a harmony, a set of common characteristics, rising perhaps out of a common confrontation of common experience, or, if it is too much to expect *identity*, are there perhaps analogies and agreements, a sharing and an equitable distribution of common possessions and responsibilities, so that Canada is really a nation as certainly as the ethnically and geographically even more diverse United States?

These questions will have to be left to the consensus of opinion formed by readers and critics. The editor's opinion perhaps finds expression in the pieces of literature he has chosen to include, though his criterion has been in every case literary, not social, political, or historical. He believes, however, that the genuine, deep, and therefore significant emotions and ideas are the ones that produce works of art of permanent value, whether in poetry or prose, painting, music, or architecture, and conversely therefore it is from art in all its forms that the true essence, *soul*, if you will, of a country can best be discerned (*CC*, p. xx).

Although he is a little evasive (as most Canadians are) on the subject of Canadian identity, Smith indicates here the true nature of the anthologist's task, a task shared also by the poet and literary critic, which is to present an insight, if his anthology be a national one, into his nation's *soul*. This is surely what tradition is about. A nation discovers its soul, even a young nation like Canada, by continuous shared experience. Of course, this might involve conflict such as that between French- and English-Canada, but so long as conflict is resolved continuity can be maintained and the soul of the country be allowed to develop and flourish. Tradition, of course, means the maintenance of continuity, a love and respect for the past and its customs as well as for the present. A country without a tradition can have no soul. And this is why A. J. M. Smith as poet, critic, and anthologist has spent his literary career in establishing, fostering, and sharpening a sense of Canadian tradition. To be an anthologist in the best sense means to be a perceiver of the soul of selected works and even the soul of a national literature. Northern simplicity, modesty, and graceful diffidence are qualities that Smith has found at the heart of Canadian literature. They also lie at the heart of his own work.

CHAPTER 5

Towards a Tradition of Canadian Letters: Conclusion

WHAT then is A. J. M. Smith's place and significance in the developing tradition of Canadian literature? As a poet, he does not regard himself as major; instead, he sees himself as a minor poet within the Canadian tradition. Together with his collaborator and friend, F. R. Scott, he spearheaded the modern movement in Canadian poetry. If the virtues of Scott and Smith were combined in the work of a single poet we might, indeed, have a major figure among the Canadian poets. Together they have made a major contribution to Canadian poetry even if separately we regard them as minor poets.

Apart from the concerns outlined earlier, Smith in his poetry shows a preoccupation with formal perfection and with technical excellence. When the future anthologist of Canadian poetry arrives at Smith's work he will have before him such poems as the ones we have praised in our discussion: "Like an Old Proud King in a Parable," "The Two Birds," "To Hold in a Poem," "Sea Cliff," "The Lonely Land," "The Circle," "The Fountain," and "Epitaph." Smith's *Poems: New & Collected* is a work of care and restraint. Like Robert Graves, he has culled his poems carefully and sought to leave behind him a canon that will do justice both to a developing Canadian poetic tradition and to his own critical ideals.

Smith's poetry and criticism, like T. S. Eliot's, are closely related. What Eliot and F. R. Leavis sought to do for the tradition of English poetry, Smith sought to do for the tradition of Canadian poetry. He has sought as critic and anthologist to sort the wheat from the chaff, to indicate the strong contours in the development of Canadian poetry. His work as an anthologist is a legacy of real worth to his country that has helped to increase the consideration

131

of Canadian poetry outside Canada. Smith knows very well that only the best work will attract the attention of the world.

There is no one in the tradition of Canadian literature quite like A. J. M. Smith. His distinctiveness results from his equal respect for poetry and criticism. No Canadian poet in English has taken literary criticism as seriously as Smith has, nor has any Canadian critic had such high standards of literary excellence. Some might argue that his devotion to criticism and his work as an anthologist of Canadian letters has limited his production as a poet. But Smith has always preferred quality to quantity. Canadian writers have, when they have attended to him, benefitted from this concern of Smith's. He is a critical conscience (one of the few Canadian literature has); his original standards of excellence are the ones we know we have to try to attain. The Canadian writer who seeks major importance will have to pay the same attention to literary criticism that Smith has paid, and will have to develop the capacity for practical self-criticism that Smith has displayed. As Smith has said, those in Canada who write in English have to see themselves as being in "open competition with the whole English-writing world" (*TVCL*, 178).

"Something whole / that was broken" are the last two lines of Smith's poem "Beside One Dead" (*Poems: New & Collected*, 149) and they refer to the risen Christ. They also remind us of the broken strength that is still strong in his best known poem "The Lonely Land." Perhaps in a consideration of Smith's work as a whole we could also see them referring to the reintegration of personality which is one of his central themes, and finally, in relation to our concern here, to the restoration of the essential and necessary bond between criticism and poetry. "Poetry," Smith has said, is "the art that most directly and intimately expresses and evaluates the compulsions of life and its environment" (*TVCL*, 3). He might have said the same of literary criticism.

Notes and References

Chapter One

1. A. J. M. Smith, "The Confessions of a Compulsive Anthologist," *Journal of Canadian Studies*, XI, 2 (May, 1976), p. 4.
2. Munro Beattie, "Poetry 1920-1935," *Literary History of Canada*, ed., Carl F. Klinck (Toronto: University of Toronto Press, 1976), II, p. 235.
3. A. J. M. Smith, *Towards a View of Canadian Letters: Selected Critical Essays 1928-71* (Vancouver: University of British Columbia Press, 1973), p. 161. Page references to this volume are supplied in brackets after quotations, following the abbreviation *TVCL*.
4. F. R. Scott, "Canadian Authors Meet," *Selected Poems* (Toronto: Oxford University Press, 1966), p. 70.
5. Sandra Djwa, "A. J. M. Smith: Of Metaphysics and Dry Bones," paper read at "A. J. M. Smith: A Symposium," Michigan State University, May 8, 1976.
6. Leon Edel, "When McGill Modernized Canadian Literature" in *The McGill You Knew*, forthcoming from Longman Canada Limited, quoted by Germaine Warkentin, "Criticism And The Whole Man," *Canadian Literature*, 64 (Spring, 1975), p. 83.
7. Louis Dudek and Michael Gnarowski, eds., *The Making of Modern Poetry in Canada* (Toronto: Ryerson Press, 1967), p. 24.
8. See Peter Stevens, ed., *The McGill Movement: A. J. M. Smith, F. R. Scott and Leo Kennedy* (Toronto: Ryerson Press, 1969).
9. Smith, "The Confessions of a Compulsive Anthologist," p. 11.

Chapter Two

1. "A. J. M. Smith" *League of Canadian Poets Catalogue of Members*, p. 110.
2. A. J. M. Smith, *Poems: New & Collected* (Toronto: Oxford University Press, 1967) is the text for the ensuing discussion of Smith's poetry. Page references to this volume will be given in brackets after all quotations from Smith's poetry.
3. See Andrew Brink, *Loss and Symbolic Repair: A Psychological Study of Some English Poets* (Hamilton, Ontario: Cromlech, 1977).
4. W. H. Auden, "In Memory of W. B. Yeats," in *Collected Shorter Poems, 1927-1957* (London: Faber, 1966), p. 143.
5. Émile Nelligan, "Le Vaisseau d'or," *The Oxford Book of Canadian*

Poetry in English and French, ed. A. J. M. Smith (Toronto: Oxford University Press, 1960), p. 131.

6. For a discussion of the three versions of the poem see Desmond Pacey, *Ten Canadian Poets* (Toronto: Ryerson, 1958), pp. 211-15 and my essay "Something Whole That Was Broken: The Poetry and Criticism of A. J. M. Smith," *Bulletin of Canadian Studies* II,; (April 1978), pp. 16-32.

7. A. J. M. Smith, ed. *The Worldly Muse: An Anthology of Serious Light Verse* (New York: Abelard Press, 1951).

8. A. J. M. Smith, "*Studies in the Metaphysical Poets of the Anglican Church in the Seventeenth Century*," Diss. University of Edinburgh 1931.

Chapter Three

1. A. J. M. Smith, *Towards a View of Canadian Letters*, p. 3. Page references will be given in brackets after all quotations from this volume.

2. W. D. Lighthall, the nineteenth-century Canadian anthologist, editor of *Songs of the Great Dominion* (1889).

3. Northrop Frye, "La tradition narrative dans la poésie canadienne-anglaise," *Gants du ciel*, 11 (Spring, 1946), pp. 19-30.

4. Milton Wilson, paper read before A.C.U.T.E. conference at Edmonton, June, 1958, printed as " 'Other Canadians' and After," *Tamarack Review*, 9 (Autumn 1958), pp. 77-92.

5. E. H. Dewart, *Selections from Canadian Poets* (Montreal: John Lovell, 1864).

6. Smith, "The Confessions of a Compulsive Anthologist," p. 6.

7. For references to a discussion of the three versions of the poem see note 6 of Chapter 2.

Chapter Four

1. Smith, "The Confessions of a Compulsive Anthologist," pp. 4-14.

2. *Ibid.*, p. 4.

3. *Ibid.*, p. 11.

4. *Ibid.*, p. 5. See also Dudek and Gnarowski, eds., *The Making of Modern Poetry in Canada*.

5. Smith, "The Confessions of a Compulsive Anthologist," pp. 5-6. Page references for subsequent quotations from the essay will be given in brackets after the abbreviation *CCA*.

6. "Yet we cannot feel that Sangster succeeded in becoming a national poet; and the reason is, I believe, that he was not first a local poet." Smith, *Towards a View of Canadian Letters*, p. 36.

7. John Sutherland, "Introduction to *Other Canadians*" in *The Making of Modern Poetry in Canada* eds. Dudek and Gnarowski, pp. 47-62.

8. Smith, *Towards a View of Canadian Letters*, pp. 161-62.

9. *Ibid.*, pp. 37-46.

10. "Introduction," *The Blasted Pine: An Anthology of Satire, Invective, and Disrespectful Verse,* eds. A. J. M. Smith and F. R. Scott (Toronto: Macmillan, 1957), p. xiii.

11. *Ibid.,* p. 117.

12. A. J. M. Smith, "Preface," *The Canadian Century* (Toronto: Gage, 1973).

Selected Bibliography

Within each section of the Bibliography items appear chronologically according to the date of publication.

PRIMARY SOURCES

A. J. M. Smith papers, University of Toronto Library.

1. Poetry

New Provinces. Poems of Several Authors. eds. F. R. Scott and A. J. M. Smith. Toronto: Macmillan, 1936.
News of the Phoenix and Other Poems. Toronto: Ryerson, 1943.
A Sort of Ecstasy. Poems: New and Selected. Toronto: Ryerson, 1954.
Collected Poems. Toronto: Oxford University Press, 1962.
Poems: New & Collected. Toronto: Oxford University Press, 1967.
The Classic Shade: Selected Poems. Toronto: McClelland and Stewart, 1978.

2. Editor

The Book of Canadian Poetry: A Critical and Historical Anthology. University of Chicago Press, 1943. 2nd revised and enlarged edition, Toronto: Gage, 1948; 3rd edition with further revisions, Toronto: Gage, 1957.
The Worldly Muse: An Anthology of Serious Light Verse. New York: Abelard Press, 1951.
The Blasted Pine: An Anthology of Satire, Invective, and Disrespectful Verse. Eds., A. J. M. Smith and F. R. Scott. Toronto: Macmillan, 1957. Revised and enlarged edition, Toronto: Macmillan, 1967.
The Oxford Book of Canadian Verse: In English and French. Toronto: Oxford University Press, 1960.
Masks of Fiction: Canadian Critics on Canadian Prose. Toronto: McClelland, 1961.
Masks of Poetry: Canadian Critics on Canadian Verse. Toronto: McClelland, 1962.
The Book of Canadian Prose, Volume I, Early Beginnings to Confederation. Toronto: Gage, 1965.
Modern Canadian Verse In English and French. Toronto: Oxford University Press, 1967.

136

The Collected Poems of Anne Wilkinson, and a Prose Memoir. Toronto: Macmillan, 1968.
The Canadian Century: English-Canadian Writing Since Confederation. Toronto: Gage, 1973. (Volume II of *The Book of Canadian Prose.*)

3. *Articles and Reviews*

"Symbolism in Poetry." *McGill Fortnightly Review*, 5 Dec. 1925, pp. 11-12 and 16.

"Hamlet in Modern Dress." *McGill Fortnightly Review* 3 Nov. 1926, pp. 2-4.

"Contemporary Poetry." *McGill Fortnightly Review* 15 Dec. 1926, pp. 31-32.

"Wanted—Canadian Criticism." *Canadian Forum*, VIII (April 1928), pp. 600-01.

"A Note on Metaphysical Poetry." *Canadian Mercury*, I (Feb. 1929), pp. 61-62.

"On Marianne Moore." *The Rocking Horse*, II, 4 (Summer, 1935).

"Canadian Poetry—Past and Present." *University of Toronto Quarterly*, 8 (Oct. 1938), p. 10.

"Canadian Poetry—A Minority Report." *University of Toronto Quarterly*, 8 (Jan. 1939), pp. 125-38.

"A Poet Young and Old—W. B. Yeats." *University of Toronto Quarterly*, VIII, 3 (April, 1939), pp. 255-63.

"Canadian Literature." *The Times*, London, May 15, 1939, "Canada Number," p. xxi.

"Canadian Anthologies, New and Old." *University of Toronto Quarterly*, 11 (July, 1942), pp. 457-74.

" 'Our Poets'—a Sketch of Canadian Poetry in the Nineteenth Century." *University of Toronto Quarterly*, 12 (October, 1942), pp. 75-94.

"Colonialism and Nationalism in Canadian Poetry before Confederation." *Report of the Canadian Historical Association*, 1944, pp. 74-85. Reprinted in *Towards a View of Canadian Letters* (1973).

"Critics and Biographers." *Canadian Historical Review*, XXV, 2 (June, 1944), pp. 196-97. Reprinted in *On Poetry and Poets.*

"Nationalism and Canadian Poetry." *Northern Review*, I, 1 (Dec., 1945-Jan., 1946), pp. 33-34.

"Abraham Moses Klein." *Gants du ciel*, 11 (Spring, 1946), pp. 67-81.

"The Poetry of Duncan Campbell Scott." *Dalhousie Review*, XXVIII (April, 1948), pp. 12-21.

"The Refining Fire: The Meaning and Use of Poetry." *Queen's Quarterly* LXI (Autumn, 1954), pp. 353-64.

"The Recent Poetry of Irving Layton." *Queen's Quarterly*, LXII, 4 (Winter, 1956), pp. 587-91.

"The Poet." *Writing in Canada*, ed. George Whalley. Toronto: Macmillan, 1956, pp. 13-24.

"A Garland for E. J. Pratt." *Tamarack Review*, 6 (Winter, 1958), pp. 66-71.

"Duncan Campbell Scott: A Reconsideration." *Canadian Literature*, I
    (Summer, 1959), pp. 13-25.
"Duncan Campbell Scott." *Our Living Tradition*, Third Series, ed. R. L.
    McDougall. Toronto: University of Toronto Press, 1959, pp. 73-94.
"Graham Greene's Theological Thrillers." *Queen's Quarterly*, LXVIII, 1
    (Spring, 1961), pp. 15-33.
"Eclectic Detachment." *Canadian Literature*, 9 (Summer, 1961), pp. 6-14.
    Reprinted in *Towards a View of Canadian Letters*.
"A Reading of Anne Wilkinson." *Canadian Literature*, 10 (Autumn, 1961),
    pp. 32-39. Reprinted in *Towards a View of Canadian Letters*.
"A Self-Review." *Canadian Literature*, 15 (Winter, 1963), pp. 20-26. Re-
    printed in *Towards a View of Canadian Letters*.
"The Critic's Task: Frye's Latest Work." *Canadian Literature*, 20 (Spring,
    1964), pp. 6-14.
"The Poet and the Nuclear Crisis." *English Poetry in Quebec*, Montreal:
    McGill University Press, 1965, pp. 13-28.
"A Rejected Preface." *Canadian Literature*, 24 (Spring, 1965), pp. 6-9.
    Reprinted in *Towards a View of Canadian Letters*.
"What is Light Verse?" from article "Light Verse." *Encyclopedia of Poetry
    and Poetics*, ed. A Preminger, Princeton University Press, 1965, pp.
    446-49.
"A Unified Personality: Birney's Poems." *Canadian Literature*, 30 (Autumn,
    1966), pp. 4-13. Reprinted in *Towards a View of Canadian Letters*.
"Pope, *The Rape of the Lock*" and "Housman, Selections from *A Shropshire
    Lad.*" *Master Poems of the English Language*, ed. O. Williams, New
    York: Trident Press, pp. 285-89 and pp. 829-30.
"Canadian Literature: The First Ten Years," *Canadian Literature*, 41
    (Summer, 1969), pp. 97-103.
"The Poetry of P. K. Page," *Canadian Literature*, 50 (Autumn, 1971), pp.
    17-27.
Towards a View of Canadian Letters. Selected Critical Essays, 1928-1971.
    Vancouver: University of British Columbia Press, 1973.
"Confessions of a Compulsive Anthologist," *Journal of Canadian Studies*, XI,
    2 (May, 1976), pp. 4-14.
On Poetry and Poets. Toronto: McClelland and Stewart (New Canadian
    Library), 1977.

SECONDARY SOURCES

1. *Articles, Studies, Reviews*

BILSLAND, JOHN. "Moving beyond Borders," Review of *The Oxford Book of
    Canadian Verse, Canadian Literature*, 6 (Autumn, 1960), pp. 56-59.
    Speaks of *OBCV* as "a valuable collection," but takes issue with Smith's
    idea of "eclectic detachment." A sensible review.
BIRNEY, EARLE. "A. J. M. S." *Canadian Literature*, 15 (Winter, 1963), pp.

4-6. Speaks of Smith's importance as "both historian and shaper of our literature."

BRINNIN, JOHN MALCOLM. "Views of Favourite Mythologies," *Poetry*, LXV (Dec., 1944), pp. 157-60. Speaks of Smith's "unsentimental irony" but finds his poetic canon lacking in unity.

BROWN, E. K. "Canadian Poetry Repudiated: Review of *New Provinces*," *New Frontier*, I (July, 1936), pp. 31-32.

————. Review of *News of the Phoenix, University of Toronto Quarterly*, XIII (April, 1944), pp. 308-10. Says that "Mr. Smith is an exigent critic. . . . Such exigence has been rare in our literature; and this shining example may be educative."

————. "A. J. M. Smith and the Poetry of Pride." *Manitoba Arts Review*, 4 (Spring, 1944), pp. 30-32. Stresses the coldness and severity of Smith's poetry.

COLLIN, W. E. "Difficult, Lonely Music." *The White Savannahs*. Toronto: Macmillan, 1936, pp. 235-63. The first extended introduction to Smith's work.

————. "Arthur Smith," *Gants du Ciel*, 11 (Spring, 1946), pp. 47-60. An introduction in French to Smith's work which stresses his connection to the Metaphysical and modern poetic traditions.

DUDEK, LOUIS. "A Load of New Books: Review of Smith's *Collected Poems*," *Delta*, 20 (Feb., 1963), pp. 27-28. Sympathetic notice of *Collected Poems* (1962).

FULLER, ROY. "A Poet of the Century," *Canadian Literature*, 15 (Winter, 1963), pp. 7-10. Presents Smith's *Collected Poems* as "despite its spareness, among the most distinguished, I believe, of the century."

GNAROWSKI, MICHAEL. "The Role of the Little Magazine in the Development of Poetry in English in Montreal," *Culture*, XXIV (September, 1963), pp. 274-86. Provides useful background information.

GUY, E. F. "Review of Smith's *Collected Poems*," *Dalhousie Review*, 43 (Autumn, 1963), pp. 437-41. Speaks of the difficulty of Smith's verse.

HUGHES, PETER. "The Singers of Vinland: Review of Smith's *Collected Poems*," *Alphabet*, 6 (June, 1963), pp. 63-64. Argues that "A. J. M. Smith is most like Robert Graves in being always himself."

KEARNS, LIONEL. "If There's Anything I Hate It's Poetry." *Canadian Literature*, 36 (Spring, 1968), pp. 67-70. Review of *Poems: New & Collected*. A hostile account of Smith's work.

KLEIN, A. M. "The Poetry of A. J. M. Smith," *Canadian Forum*, XXIII (February, 1944), pp. 257-58. Speaks of Smith's high standards, self-criticism, and classicism.

LIVESAY, DOROTHY. Review of *News of the Phoenix, First Statement*, II (April, 1944), pp. 18-19.

MATHEWS, ROBIN. "Canadian Poetry and Fiction: Review of Smith's *Collected Poems*," *Queen's Quarterly*, 70 (Summer, 1963), pp. 282-83. Says that Smith's verse lacks humanity.

McCallum, Faye Maureen. "To Capture Proteus: A Study of the Poetry and Critical Work of A. J. M. Smith," M.A. Thesis, Queen's University, 1971. A useful study of Smith's poetry and criticism.

New, William H. "A Search for Sensibility." Review of *The Book of Canadian Prose: Volume I, Early Beginnings to Confederation, Canadian Literature*, 27 (Winter, 1966), pp. 63-65. Considers the difficulties involved in creating such a book.

O'Broin, Padraig. "After Strange Gods (A. J. M. Smith and the Concept of Nationalism)," *Canadian Author and Bookman*, 39 (Summer, 1964), pp. 6-8. Presents Smith as a "cosmopolitan" and an "exile."

Pacey, Desmond. "A. J. M. Smith." *Ten Canadian Poets*. Toronto: Ryerson, 1958, pp. 194-222. A useful study.

Schultz, Gregory Peter. "The Periodical Poetry of A. J. M. Smith, F. R. Scott, Leo Kennedy, A. M. Klein and Dorothy Livesay, 1925-1950," M.A. Thesis, University of Western Ontario, 1957.

Scott, F. R. Letter in Reply to "Wanted—Canadian Criticism," *Canadian Forum*, VIII (June, 1928), pp. 697-98. Argues that Canadian literature cannot be forced into existence.

———. "A. J. M. Smith," *Leading Canadian Poets*, ed. W. P. Percival. Toronto: Ryerson, 1948, pp. 234-44. Presents Smith as the man who introduced modernism to Canada.

Shaw, Neufville. "The Maple Leaf is Dying, A Review of Smith's *Book of Canadian Poetry*," *Preview*, 17 (Dec., 1943), pp. 1-3.

Skelton, Robin. "Canadian Poetry?: Review of Smith's *Collected Poems*," *Tamarack Review*, 29 (Autumn, 1963), pp. 75-76. Says that Smith's verse "combines a deep feeling for romantic symbolism with a shrewd distrust of the pretentious."

Stephens, Donald. "Old Canadians Renewed," Review of *Masks of Fiction*, *Canadian Literature*, 12 (Spring, 1962), p. 83. A very brief review.

Stevens, Peter. ed. *The McGill Movement: A. J. M. Smith, F. R. Scott, and Leo Kennedy*. Toronto: Ryerson, 1969, pp. 95-143. The most useful secondary source where some of the best of these articles and reviews can be found.

Sutherland, John. "The Two Schools," *First Statement*, II (August, 1943), pp. 1-3.

———. "Literary Colonialism," *First Statement*, II, 3 (February, 1944).

———. Review of Smith's *Book of Canadian Poetry*, *First Statement*, II (April, 1944), pp. 19-20. Notes the limitations of "cosmopolitanism."

———. "The Old and The New," Introduction to *Other Canadians*, Montreal: First Statement Press, 1947, pp. 5-20. Argues that Smith prefers the "cosmopolitan" to the "native" tradition.

Symons, Julian. "A National Style?" *Canadian Literature*, 36 (Spring, 1968), pp. 58-61. A review of *Modern Canadian Verse* which argues that Canadian poetry, though confident, lacks "a truly national style."

WARKENTIN, GERMAINE. "Criticism and the Whole Man," *Canadian Literature*, 64 (Spring, 1975), pp. 83-91. A highly critical account of Smith's contribution to Canadian literature.

WILSON, MILTON. "Poetry: Review of Smith's *Collected Poems*," *University of Toronto Quarterly*, XXXII (July, 1963), pp. 371-73. Stresses Smith's restraint and spareness.

————. "Second and Third Thoughts about Smith," *Canadian Literature*, 15 (Winter, 1963), pp. 11-17. Discusses Smith's concern for purity both as a critic and a poet.

WOODCOCK, GEORGE. "Smith's Hundred," *Canadian Literature*, 15 (Winter, 1963), p. 3. Editorial introducing *Canadian Literature*'s "Salute to A. J. M. Smith."

————. "Turning New Leaves." *Canadian Forum*, XLII (February, 1963), pp. 257-58. Sees Smith as "among the more memorable lyric poets writing in our time, not merely in Canada, but in the whole English-speaking world."

————. "Two Aspects of A. J. M. Smith: 1. The Poet, 2. Anthology as Epithalamion." *Odysseus Ever Returning*. Toronto: McClelland and Stewart, 1970, pp. 111-18. A useful introduction to Smith's work as poet and anthologist.

2. *Papers read at Michigan State University Symposium on A. J. M. Smith, May, 1976*

DJWA, SANDRA. "A. J. M. Smith: Of Metaphysics and Dry Bones."

EDEL, LEON. "Mr. Smith and his Worldly Muse: a Critical Homage."

MANDEL, ELI. "Masks of Criticism."

ROSENTHAL, M.L. "Poor Innocent: the Poetry of A. J. M. Smith." This was published in *Modern Poetry Studies*, 8 (Spring, 1977), and became the Introduction to *The Classic Shade: Selected Poems of A. J. M. Smith*. Toronto: McClelland and Stewart, 1978, pp. 9-19.

Index